MY SO-CALLED LIFE AS A
SUBMISSIVE WIFE

MY SO-CALLED LIFE AS A
SUBMISSIVE WIFE

SARA HORN

HARVEST HOUSE PUBLISHERS
EUGENE, OREGON

Cover design by Dugan Design Group, Bloomington, Minnesota

Cover photo © Serg Zastavkin / Shutterstock

The author is represented by the literary agency of Alive Communications, Inc., 7680 Goddard Street, Suite 200, Colorado Springs, CO 80920. www.alivecommunications.com.

This book contains some stories in which the author has changed people's names and some details of their situations in order to protect their privacy.

My So-Called Life as a Submissive Wife
Copyright © 2013 by Sara Horn
Published by Harvest House Publishers
Eugene, Oregon 97402
www.harvesthousepublishers.com

Library of Congress Cataloging-in-Publication Data
Horn, Sara, 1977-
My so-called life as a submissive wife / Sara Horn.
    pages cm
    ISBN 978-0-7369-5283-5 (pbk.)
    ISBN 978-0-7369-5284-2 (eBook)
    1. Wives—Religious life. 2. Submissiveness—Religious aspects—Christianity. 3. Horn, Sara, 1977- I. Title.
    BV4528.15.H674 2013
    248.8'435—dc23

2013002888

Printed in the United States of America
        13 14 15 16 17 18 19 20 21 22 / VP-JH / 10 9 8 7 6 5 4 3 2 1

To Cliff:

I am so grateful for the story
God continues to write for us,
and the journey He's put us on together.

Acknowledgments

Writing a personal narrative or a memoir like this is not just personal; it can also be very challenging because more often than not, other people's stories are included as well.

First, I want to say a big thank you to my husband, Cliff, for his willingness to take on another "experiment" with me and for the growth we've seen in our marriage and the impact God has made on our relationships with Him as well as each other.

I also thank my in-laws, Ray and Nancy Horn, my mom Gail, and the rest of our extended family and friends for their patience and agreement to let me include them in our story.

Special thanks must go to my editor, Rod Morris, for his enduring patience and encouragement as we went through the editing process. It has been wonderful working on this second project with you, and I'm looking forward to others in the future!

I also extend a grateful thank you to Larae Weikert, Barb Sherrill, and the entire Harvest House staff for all of your support. I truly feel like I am part of an exceptional, wonderful team, and I am so grateful.

A big thank you also to my agent, Andrea Heinecke, and Alive Communications. Thank you Andrea for accepting my panicked phone calls and always knowing what to say to help this crazy writer finally hit the send button!

To my incredible team of leaders and friends at Wives of Faith—thank you for your support!

To my readers, it is such a joy to walk this journey with you. I never take for granted the emails and contacts I receive from you, and when I hear that one of my books has encouraged you to grow in your relationship with God or to take steps to improve your marriage or your family, I immediately whisper a thankful prayer to God for giving me the opportunity. Thank you for letting me be real with you and thank you for being real with me.

Finally, I am so grateful to God for what he has done in my life. *Through the hardships, the challenges, the blessings and the joys, you have shown me that the only thing that matters is you. Please continue to help me grow closer to you and stay discerning to your will.*

Why I Don't Want You to Read This Book

This book is not for everyone. Seriously.

No, please don't think, *Oh, she's using reverse psychology on me,* or *She went to some author marketing class where the instructor and all of the wannabe writers sat around plotting and saying if we tell them not to buy, they're gonna want to buy!*

Um, no.

I truly and honestly don't want you to read or buy this book if it's not for you.

I can think of at least two types of people who do not need to read this book. These include women who already feel like they have a strong grasp on what it means to be submissive to their husbands (awesome, congrats, very happy for you), and women who are looking for a clear, concise guide or handbook with steps, charts, and footnotes on what it means to be submissive to their husbands (awesome, congrats, and good luck with that).

If you fit in the former group, you will probably be bored to yawns when you read what I have to say and not enjoy it very much or feel like you get anything out of it. You will probably call me immature or naive or believe I have a lot more living I need to do. If you are in the latter group, you will probably be frustrated and not enjoy it very much and want your money back. You will probably say I'm a terrible writer or teacher and I should never attempt to write anything else again. Noted.

So, either way, let me save you the time and the cash and give you permission to walk away now. Before you get upset with me and post a nasty review online saying you already know more about this topic than I do, or you were looking for a how-to guide and this was more of a story, maybe a nice story, maybe a slightly interesting story, but not what you were looking for, and not very helpful.

There. I've already said it for you. Please find a book that will be a better fit and save us both some frustration.

I hope you're reading this online as a preview. But if you're not, if you're holding this book in your hands, just take it back, send it back, give it back. The only word of caution I offer is if someone else gave it to you as a gift—a friend, a sister, a mom—then maybe, just maybe, you might want to give it a chance. They could have a better idea than you do at this moment for why you should read it.

I stand by everything I just stated with one exception—if your *husband* is the gift-giver of this book. And you didn't ask for it. You haven't heard of it. This is the first time you're seeing it. And just because of the title, if you know nothing else about this book, or about me, and you're feeling a little annoyed at your spouse right now, maybe a little frustrated, quite likely wondering if you've just been insulted or told something you don't want to hear, or aren't ready to hear…If that's the case, then you definitely have my permission to do one very important thing with this book before you give it back.

Hit him with it.

Sorry it's not a hardcover. I recommend two hands.

If, however, you *don't* fit in these two categories, then please, by all means, keep reading. Because I'd like to tell you why I wrote this in the first place.

I think how-to books are great. Books that fit the Christian living genre are also wonderful. They're inspiring and offer refreshing guidance, hopefully based on what Scripture says. I have written a couple of books in that category. I've read many, many more that I've loved and that helped me gain new perspective in areas where I needed it.

But I also believe in the power of story. And I think sometimes, for some people, seeing your own story in someone else's can be much more educational and inspirational and effective than reading someone else's words telling you if you do A and B, you will definitely see X. Because sometimes, when you dutifully follow A and B and you don't see X, or X shows up in a different way, at a different time or in blue instead of green, or with a lot more tears and frustration than what the original X-promoter said would happen, well you start feeling as confused as you probably do trying to read this last sentence.

I discovered some things about the power of story when I wrote my previous book, *My So-Called Life as a Proverbs 31 Wife*. This was a very different book for me to write, and it required me to step out of my normal writing comfort zone. It's my story of a year-long experiment I attempted while trying to figure out who I was as a wife and mom in the context of who the Proverbs 31 wife was. And the kind of wife and mom God wanted me to be.

It's very personal. It's extremely honest. I had no idea what women would think about it. I didn't know what they'd think about me.

But after the book was released, gently tugged from my trembling fingers by the publisher to be received by tens of thousands, I heard from a lot of you. What blessed me so much was that in your emails and Facebook messages and Twitter mentions, there was often a common repeated theme. You appreciated the real, the honest, the little peek into my life amidst the raw, and you were challenged to look closer into your own lives. You told me you saw need of change for yourself, in your day-to-day interactions with your family, in the way you handled things in your marriage, things you needed to do differently, minor or major shifts you needed to make with certain mindsets, in various habits, in specific approaches. I loved hearing about those, especially when you told me how the changes you made impacted your family for the good.

And even better? I was never the one who told you to make them.

That's what I love, and what I mean, about the power of story. God uses our stories to help others shape and change their own stories into what he wants them to be. Not what someone else thinks or says your story should be. And that's honestly at the heart of what I hope and pray for this new story you hold in your hands.

We've increased the threat level on this one, haven't we? The button's bright red and glowing (or glaring, depending on your perspective) to be pushed. Submission is not a feel-good topic like how to cook better or ways to clean faster or how to not lock up your kids or kill your husband when you're a wife and mom trying to follow Proverbs 31. At least there are many individuals and groups and even ministries of Christian women who love and embrace the Proverbs 31 wife.

Submission is a different story. There's a lot more eye-rolling with this one. It's different. More sensitive. More intrusive. The stakes just *feel* a whole lot higher, like your very right to breathe as a woman is on the line. You won't find a lot of Pinterest pins with a cartoonish drawing of a smiling woman and the words "A submissive wife is a happy wife!"

The truth is, women in droves have passed by this book in the bookstore and just kept walking, insulted for even seeing this word in a Christian context. We'll pick up steamy novels all about doing exactly what a man wants us to in the context of submission in sex, but refer to submission in the context of a spiritual perspective? That's just old-fashioned and far behind our culture today. Right? Shades of grey? I would say so.

But you, my dear, didn't keep walking. You did pick this up or download it or borrow it, as the case may be. For whatever reason. So here's the deal. This word *submission* is in the Bible. Not once but several times. So as much as we sometimes want to ignore it, I don't think we can. I don't believe we should. Not if we're following Christ. Not if we're committed to living honorable and righteous lives that spill out in the highways and byways of our marriages and our families. Eventually we've got to address this ten-letter word that so often comes across as a four-letter one. At some point, we have to decide for ourselves how we feel about this topic that seems to make people cringe the same way they do when they accidentally take a swig of sour milk.

Let me make this even more personal. Eventually, in my marriage, in my walk with God, I have to face this whole submission idea. I have to say, am I for it? Or against it? Am I voting yay or nay? Whether I intentionally try to ignore it or not, whether I try to pretend it doesn't exist…through my actions, I declare my intentions. I accept it or I don't.

It's time to stop ignoring this word we've all decided, or at least culture at large has decided, is so ugly, whether we know why we think that way or not. We need to understand what this whole concept of submission looks like and what it means in life and marriage and in relation to God's plan for everything.

But it's not up to me to decide what that looks like.

If I approach the Bible as my spiritual authority, as God's Word, this Book that's been around for so many thousands of years, that what it says truly goes, then don't I need to understand it? And apply it?

Not as my interpretation based on what I feel at the time, but an interpretation based on what the Bible actually says? Taking it at full value, not twisting it to suit my needs and my temperament in the moment?

And so we go back to the power of the story. Story gives you insight and information and sometimes even knowledge, but often it also simultaneously forces questions to be asked. Questions that get raised when

you suddenly put yourself in someone else's shoes and you start to wonder the more you read…

"Am I doing that?"

"Should I do that?"

"Why couldn't I do that?"

I ask a lot of questions in my stories. Readers don't always like that
because it's easier sometimes when you see only answers. At least it feels
easier. Questions make you think. Thinking can be hard. Especially when
it comes to the heart.

My prayer, though, is that as you read through this story, you'll be willing to think. You'll be open to visualizing yourself attempting an "experiment" in biblical submission. Experiments, by the way, feel a little less
ominous. A little less permanent. You're trying it out the way you might
try out a new bottle of nail polish or a new bedspread. But what happens
when you allow yourself to try is that you open yourself to see the possibilities of life-changing attitudes. You're more open to applying principles from Proverbs 31 or being more intentional in showing honor and
respect to your husband, whereas before, you might have held yourself
back because of your already-formed perceptions. And often, like experiments do, you discover something you weren't expecting.

Maybe you'll sympathize with, maybe you'll satirize, what I've written
within these pages. But my hope is by the end of this book, by the end of
this story, you'll find yourself reflecting. Looking within your own marriage, your own family, and your own Bible, thinking about changes, if
any, you need to make in your life and in your relationship with your husband. And most important, your relationship with God.

If none of this sounds good to you, then let me kindly say good-bye
and thanks for the moment of your time. But if this has tapped something inside you, something that may feel like a deep cavity that needs to
be filled, or at least examined, then please keep reading.

There's a whole lot more ahead.

Submission in Abusive Marriages

I am sensitive to the fact that every marriage is different, and while there are many solid marriage relationships out there based on godly principles and a strong Christian foundation, where both the husband and the wife love each other and desire to serve God and each other, I also realize there are other relationships where that is sadly, and heartbreakingly, not the case. The husband defines himself as his wife's lord and master and expects her to treat him as such, misusing the Bible and abusing the responsibility and role God has given him toward his wife emotionally, physically, or both.

While I'm not sure a woman faced with this situation would even be interested in reading a book like this, one that offers a little tongue-in-cheek humor at ourselves as wives attempting to follow God's guidelines while also encouraging serious thought, if you are reading this and you are dealing with marital abuse of any kind, please find a way to get help. You may be stopping yourself from reaching out for help because you've either been convinced by your husband or other people or even by yourself that submission means to just take whatever is thrown at you—literally or figuratively. But hear this loud and clear…

It does not.

Being beaten, whether by words or fists, is not the submission God has in mind for women who are wives.*

---

* For a more complete and biblical perspective on abuse in marriage in the context of submission, visit John Piper's blog, *Desiring God* (www.desiringgod.com) and search for the article, "Clarifying Words on Wife Abuse," posted December 19, 2012.

Who Wants to
Be a Submissive Wife?

I called my husband the other day while he was at work and told him I was thinking about taking a year to study what it means to be a submissive wife and write about it.

"Would you be OK with that?" I asked.

"No," he said.

Well, that was uncharacteristically direct. (And yes, I can only assume that as you hold this book in your hands, you see the irony.)

"Why would you want to do that?" he asked me. "You and I, we work together as a team. We do things together. You're not like that. I'm not like that. That's not us."

I wasn't prepared for his reaction. I thought he'd welcome the opportunity to have me at his beck and call. I thought he'd jump at the chance to not just be the "head of household" but have my constant and immediate cooperation at all times (which is not always consistent or always immediate). I was waiting for some crack about bringing his slippers and fetching him a sweet tea—not an immediate dismissal of the entire idea.

Cliff's question made sense, though. Why would I want to do something so many in our world today see as a very old-fashioned if not archaic idea for marriage?

I've come far in our fourteen years of marriage, but you'd never mistake me for June Cleaver or Martha Washington. Two years ago I spent a year attempting to be like the Proverbs 31 wife. Though nothing went the way I planned, the experience and what I learned from it brought good changes, major changes, both in our family and in me.

God taught me during that year how much more he cares about my attitude and my desire to seek his will in my life than how many things I check off the to-do list each day. For the first time as a wife, I saw myself as the thermostat of my family and realized my actions have great influence—whether I want them to or not. The old saying, "If Mama ain't happy, ain't nobody happy," does apply. Because the opposite does too: If Mama is happy, the family also is a whole lot happier.

So, since "the Proverbs 31 experiment," as I sometimes call it, I've learned some things. I've changed some things—OK, a lot of things—in what I do as a wife and mom. I cook more. Whine less. I put my family first, though I still sometimes feel like I struggle managing everything. But I want to learn more. I want to continue growing deeper in my relationship with God. And if as a wife, God wants me to learn submission… well, I need to at least look at it a little more closely. Even if it's as painful as it sounds.

That's what I told Cliff.

But he still wasn't budging.

"OK," I pressed, "then what's your idea of a submissive wife? I mean, I'm not planning on dressing up in long jean skirts and wearing my hair down to my ankles and avoiding makeup, if that's what you're thinking." (My apologies to the ladies who do this. You look beautiful. Really.)

Silence came over the line as he thought about it. I waited.

"I guess when I think about the word *submissive*…uh…you know *Star Wars*, right?"

"Uh, yes?" I had no idea where this was going.

"Well, you know that old movie poster, with Hans Solo and Princess Leia? The one where she's like lying on the ground, all curled up around his legs? That's what I think when I think of the word *submission*."

"Seriously?" I asked, trying not to laugh. "I guess that's one of the reasons why I want to take this on. I think a lot of us have so many different ideas about what submission is—what it looks like. Some people think it's all about the man being in complete control and the little woman doing his bidding. Some think it's equal—men and women complement and complete each other and they should work together."

I paused, trying to think of the words that might go with how I was feeling at the moment.

"I guess I just want to study what the Bible says about it. And pursue that. You know what I mean?"

There was that silence again.

"Let me think about it," Cliff said.

We hung up, and I had this eerie feeling of waiting for my husband to make a decision on something I wanted to do. Was this submission? Not sure I liked it. This might be even tougher than I thought.

An hour later, my inbox chimed and it was a note from Cliff. He'd sent a link to an article he found online about biblical submission, written by a woman. It was lengthy, but she broke down the usual verses mentioned when it comes to submission, and offered her analysis:

> Submission to a husband does not mean a woman is to be a slave in bondage to that man, but rather it is to be a mutual submission in love. The above Scripture (Ephesians 5:21-33) says we are to submit unto each other. Submission means to yield or "to set yourself under." From this definition we see we are to yield to one another instead of demanding our own way. Love should be the rule in our homes, and we should "prefer one another."

My phone rang. It was Cliff, wanting to know if I'd seen the article he sent.

"I did. It's good. What did you think?" I asked.

"I think I've never really thought about it much," he said. "I think I agree with her point about mutual submission."

"See…I'm not so sure." I surprised myself a little, and probably Cliff too, because I've always seen our marriage as a 50/50 partnership. But as I've looked at the Scriptures lately, I'm not as confident. "I mean, it does say in Ephesians to submit to one another, but is that in the marriage context or in the church context? And if it's in the marriage context, then why does it say that women should submit to their husbands, and husbands are heads of their wives?"

"OK, well, I think it's interesting," Cliff said. "And I'm OK if you want to do this."

"Are you sure? It's going to affect you too—maybe not in the way you're expecting."

"Yeah, I know, and I'm OK with it. But can I make a request?"

"Sure," I said, happy we were both on the same page and excited, though nervous, to start this new experiment.

"Anytime you want to dress up as Princess Leia, you totally have my permission."

Oh, brother.

The Word No One Likes to Say

No one I know would describe my personality as "submissive." I can think of lots of examples where I've acted the opposite. Like a lot of girls in my generation, I suppose, my seventies-era parents raised me with the idea I could do whatever I wanted and be whatever I wanted...whenever I wanted it.

Strong, independent, graceful, assertive, understanding—these descriptors I prefer. Submissive sounds weak. It makes me think of the time my husband trained our dog, Sammy, to obey. Multiple times a day, Cliff rolled him over and held him down until he stopped struggling and lay still. Sammy learned to listen. He gave up his own will. He submitted to his master.

This isn't the picture I want for myself. I don't like the idea of someone else being in control. But that's how submission sounds to me at this moment. Someone else in control.

Cliff is in his sixteenth year as a Seabee with the Navy Reserves. His job is building things. We like to say Seabees fix what the Marines break. Or maybe more accurately, what the Marines blow up.

At the end of my Proverbs 31 experiment, Cliff left for his second deployment, spending ten months away from home. During the first half, he traveled by ship from port to port in countries along the South America border. The group he was with helped carry out humanitarian missions sponsored by the U.S. Navy and other supporting humanitarian organizations. I was proud of all they had accomplished, building schools and making life better for many different groups of people. The remainder of his time was at Guantánamo Bay in Cuba, starting and completing building projects for the navy base there.

That deployment was the first I'd had an opportunity to visit him—a week in Cuba shortly after our thirteenth anniversary. It was wonderful to see him after almost eight months apart, though I felt guilty for leaving our son, Caleb, behind with the grandparents.

Something else that changed was our living situation. Six months after Cliff left South Carolina for this second deployment, so did Caleb and I. We'd just moved there eight months before Cliff left, but with no close friends or family in the area, and not living in a military town, life began to feel like a seriously depressing movie loop that wouldn't quit. It was only when my in-laws came for a visit the week before Christmas that I realized Caleb and I were smiling for the first time in a month.

As God worked during that time I took to focus on being a better wife and mom, he also helped me start craving real relationships over accomplishment. So in March, with Cliff's blessing and help from family, I quit my job, packed us up, and moved us back home to a small town in South Louisiana to stay with my in-laws until Cliff came home.

This is the town where Cliff and I met. Where we married. Where both of us spent time in school. Middle and high school for him. Grade school and middle school for me. There are roots here. Roots that for many years I tried to snap off. Cliff has good memories here, but mine aren't so good. This is where my family lived too, before my parents divorced. A lot of shadows creep in around the sunshine for me. But I'm hoping time does heal old wounds.

Since we've moved back, I've discovered the joy in reconnecting with old friends, and I've made a few new ones. I've found comfort in the familiar, seeing folks from our old church who still remember me from when I was ten. Since we've lived away for almost all our married life, it's also been a change having family around once again. A lot of family. *All the time.* It's been good to not be by ourselves anymore. It's also taken some getting used to.

Cliff's sister, Kelly, and her family live just on the outskirts of town. His twin brother, Clay, has an apartment just a few minutes away. And we currently live with his parents, who I affectionately call Ms. Nancy and Mr. Ray. Since we started dating when I was just nineteen, my southern manners kept me from calling them anything else, and after we got married, it just kind of stuck. Not sure if Ms. Nancy liked it at first, but I think it's grown on her. And after more than fourteen years of calling her that, it's not changing anyway.

For the most part, living with Cliff's parents has been a blessing. I know making room for us wasn't the easiest thing to do, and everyone likes their own space. But it's harder since Cliff came home.

We went from never having anyone around to seeing people all the time. Though I enjoy meeting people and speaking to groups, I'm an introvert at heart. I recharge when I can get quiet. High-energy situations wear me out. Not having much time to myself wears me out. And now that Cliff is home, I'm longing for our own house again, our single little patch of precious ground amid all the roots where we can recharge.

Three years ago, when we lived in Nashville, Cliff lost his job as a marketing director for a Christian radio station due to budget cuts. He was let go just six months after he returned from his first deployment to Iraq. Two moves later, after two deployments and five months of being back here, he finally found a position working for the state as a public information officer. After living so long with both of us being at the house, now that he leaves for a job each day, life feels a little more normal.

If you can count three generations living under the same roof as normal.

We're blessed that the Horns have a good-sized house. Cliff and I have a bedroom, and Caleb, who is now ten, has his own room. There's another bedroom we call the home office, and Ms. Nancy ensured after we moved in that everyone had a desk in there. Tight but cozy, and I was impressed by her ingenuity. She went to the local home improvement store and bought simple sheets of plywood that she covered with black contact paper and placed over filing cabinets that offer support and storage. They look great and serve their purpose.

Since Caleb and I moved in almost a year ago, we pay rent by the month to cover food and utilities, and all of us try to share kitchen and housekeeping duties and help as much as we can.

It's impossible, though, for two moms and two wives to live under the same roof without a little friction. Only one can be the true mother hen, and Ms. Nancy certainly has earned that title in her forty-plus years of being a wife and a mom. So I try my best to mind my manners and be a help to her and not a nuisance (although I'm sure at times I'm a little of both).

I was curious how she might react when I told her what I planned to do with this whole submission experiment. Because I don't see her fitting the submissive category any more than I do. She's in charge. She has a presence that just oozes poise and confidence, but also serious control.

When Ms. Nancy speaks, you listen. When she speaks, it's with kindness and sincerity, but if she asks you to do something, you just do it. That includes her husband. Her kids. Her grandkids. You know who is in charge. Of course, she's also the first to drop everything to help someone, and she has helped many—her husband, her kids, her friends, her grandchildren, her extended family. She's like the Energizer Bunny, and some days I really wish I could find for myself whatever batteries she uses.

Her eyebrows rose slightly when I told her what I was planning, and a big grin spread across her face. "OK," she said.

"OK?" I said. "Well, do you think it's a good idea?"

She stood up from the couch in our living room and bent over, straightening newspapers on the wide black ottoman that serves as a coffee table. She looked up at me with her 100-watt smile. "I'm thinking you've never been submissive since I've known you."

My stomach tightened a little. OK, yes, she was probably right. I mean, it's one of the reasons I did the whole Proverbs 31 experiment. There was a lot I needed to learn when it came to being a wife and a mom. But did she have to write the idea off so quickly?

I persisted. "Well, what do you think about the whole submission thing? What does submission mean to you?"

She stood up and paused thoughtfully. "I think it's putting your husband first. And that's something I've always done. I put Ray first."

I couldn't argue with that. I knew she'd encouraged him to join the navy shortly after they were married, and how after he'd left the navy on a medical discharge, she worked hard to get him into school at Ole Miss while she worked in the admissions office there. She'd always put him first. Especially in recent years.

After having major surgery, Mr. Ray became antsy to travel and insisted on selling their house—the house they'd built from scratch two years earlier. This was a house Ms. Nancy had planned from the blueprints to the construction to the decorating. It was exactly as she'd wanted it. It was her dream home, and she gave it up for her husband. They sold the house and spent a year traveling off and on while staying with their son Clay when they were in town.

Eventually, Mr. Ray decided he wanted a home base after all. So now they were living in another house they'd bought, but it wasn't her dream home. Though there was no denying she was queen of her castle, it was true Ms. Nancy always worked to make things nice for her king and keep him happy. I suddenly felt as if I'd treated poor Cliff like a pawn for a lot of our years together. Or maybe a rook.

If I'm painfully honest, for much of our marriage I focused on myself. I didn't see it like that at the time; I honestly believed I worked hard to serve God and to make a difference in the world. But my hard-working passion and drive sometimes ran away from my husband's laid-back and relaxed personality. It was easy for me to lead; it was often just as easy for him to follow.

Over the years, as I saw more success in my career, it became normal for me to go forward full throttle and forget to make sure Cliff was still with me. We worked around my schedule and my plans. We moved back to Tennessee after we married to finish our degrees at the university I'd started at, and we moved to Nashville for a job I was offered.

Though he rarely complained or said anything, eventually my work-aholic ways wore thin, and seven years into our marriage we hit our first major wall. There were problems in paradise. My drive and determination, things I'd once been so proud of, threatened to seriously damage our relationship and our family life. It took a few years for us to heal and work through the issues that came up. Though she didn't know any of this, my mother-in-law was right. My track record proved it. Submission wasn't exactly my standard for marriage.

Later that evening, I called my friend Heather. She and I met in second grade when my family moved to town the first time. We were best friends until middle school when the social caste system of seventh and eighth grade girls sent her one way and me the other. My family moved away in the middle of eighth grade, and we lost touch for many years. But after my family moved back, we reconnected in college. She was a brides-maid in my wedding; I was a bridesmaid in hers. Now that Cliff and I were back in town, hopefully for good, we were having fun becoming close friends again, now as moms of boys—me to our ten-year-old, she to her four-year-old.

Heather was honest and to the point.

"No, no. There's no way I could be like that," she said. "I think Andre and I work as a team—we work together and help each other. We both serve each other."

"I know what you mean," I said. "But I wonder maybe if there's more to it—that maybe our definition of submission and what we think it's supposed to look like is wrong. Maybe we've let culture influence us as believers more than we realize. I just want to examine what the Bible says and see if I can apply it in my marriage—and not go entirely crazy."

Heather chuckled in agreement. "Well, good luck, friend! "

My mom's response didn't surprise me. First she laughed, hard, and then in her thick southern twang, said, "Why would you want to do that?" She was half-kidding, half not as we caught up on the phone the next day. She still lived in Nashville, just a few minutes from where we used to live. After she and my dad divorced so many years earlier, she eventually moved to Tennessee to be closer to us and her grandson. Now we were in Louisiana.

If I were to size up any woman in the independent, large-and-in-charge category, it would be my mother. Part of it, I think, was out of necessity. My dad was and is a quiet, almost painfully reserved kind of guy. The men who knew him from church used to tell Mom they listened when he spoke because he never talked much to begin with, so you knew it was important when he did. Still, it made for a pretty lonely existence for my extrovert of a mother.

She made up for it by doing stuff with us kids. While my dad worked, she'd pile us three kids into the car and drive all over the country, especially during the summer, visiting friends and family. She wasn't afraid of anything, at least not in our minds. She'd move furniture and pack up and unpack houses for our several moves as a family. She was never a military wife, but she could have been. Growing up, my mom was the strongest version of a woman I knew. But not necessarily an example of a submissive wife.

"I know you always like taking on a challenge, Sara, but this one may be a little much," she said. "But I'm sure it'll be interesting to see what you discover."

I can always count on my mom to at least support, even when she doesn't always understand.

It was interesting to see such immediate reactions from everyone. After hearing all of their different responses and thoughts about this, it's clear this is a topic that's not so black-and-white. At least not in our culture.

I'm praying that spending a year working through the Proverbs 31 experiment has prepared me for this one. My priorities are certainly different. I still believe God's using me for his purpose; I'm just no longer so tunnel-visioned that I don't also see he's given me a ministry to live out with my husband and my son. And I want to put my husband first because I believe that's one of my callings as a wife.

Just over the past two years alone, God's shown me the fruits of putting my family first. Our family is happy. There's less bickering and fighting over who does what around the house. My attitude is different and because of that, our house is much more peaceful. But more than putting my family or my husband first, I want to put God first. I want to follow his plan. Not on my terms, but on his.

Living with the In-Laws

You might have a hard time guessing the ages of Cliff's parents. Though they're in their sixties now, neither one looks it. Ms. Nancy still has her girl-next-door looks, trademark smile, and sing-song "Helloooo!" that wakes up a room when she walks in. She's a model of grace and poise and confidence, and if she'd come along in any decade later than the fifties, I'm sure she would be the CEO of her own company today.

But she was born in the fifties, the fifth child of Earl and Alice Barnett, and a surprise to her parents, who were in their forties by the time she arrived. Technically, she was the fourth, but before any of them were born, her parents adopted as their own a little girl who was identified as "slow," as they called it back then. Edna Earl was several years older than Ms. Nancy, grew up as part of the family, and lived with Alice, who we all called Grandmother, until the day Grandmother passed away. (Cliff's granddaddy had died several years before.) Edna Earl then lived with Ms. Nancy until Edna herself passed away.

Taking care of people is something that seems to come naturally for Ms. Nancy since she grew up in a home where her mother cared for old folks. They lived in a tiny southern Mississippi town, and there were always a couple of rooms and a few beds filled in their house. Ms. Nancy never knew what it was like not to help others, whether family or not.

Mr. Ray lived with his family in the next town over, and the two of them met in high school. Their love story of now more than forty years almost didn't happen, though. One day Ms. Nancy called over to Mr. Ray's house to find out when he was picking her up for the school dance he'd promised to take her to that night, only to learn from his mama that he was over at another girl's house—a girl who just happened to be Ms. Nancy's best friend.

Ms. Nancy called over to where he was, and Mr. Ray mumbled something about not being able to go. "Oh, you are going to take me to this dance, Ray Horn," she told him. "I've already told my friends we're going and I already have a dress, and you will not break your promise." What she said or how she said it apparently convinced him, and he did what he was told. (When Ms. Nancy told me this story, she admitted that she didn't let him off the hook, however, once they were at the dance. She was still so mad at him, she ignored him the rest of the night.)

He must have learned his lesson, though, because there was no more waffling between two girls for my father-in-law. He and Ms. Nancy married a little over a year later, right after he graduated. Ms. Nancy graduated the year before. They are still going strong, forty-plus years later.

I love this story because it is just one example of the strength of my mother-in-law. Though she'd been able to attend college only briefly before family responsibilities kept her from finishing, Ms. Nancy put her husband through school not once but twice—once before Mr. Ray enlisted in the navy, and again when he unexpectedly had to retire due to health issues. She packed up their family and moved wherever the navy assigned them, and she served as an ombudsman for the ship Mr. Ray was assigned to. While Mr. Ray worked as an instructor for nuclear power plants the remainder of his career, she also worked various jobs, usually secretarial in nature—once at a prison, once at a paper mill, and then for several years as manager of our town's local travel agency. Always with high class and high standards and a smile on her face.

But I have to confess. At the moment, trying to live as a submissive wife to my husband while living under my in-laws' roof feels more like learning to be submissive to my in-laws. I have always loved my mother-in-law, but she's also always lived hundreds if not a few thousand miles away. Living up close and personal seven days a week, twenty-four hours a day brings you up close and personal to the good, the great, and sometimes the not so good. (I'm sure she could say the same about me.)

Both Ms. Nancy and Mr. Ray are now retired and home all the time—when they're not traveling. Ms. Nancy still works for the travel agency, only she now leads trips as a tour guide instead of managing from behind a desk. She teaches finance classes sometimes at church and occasionally to companies. When they are home, Mr. Ray keeps busy as the volunteer pool man at the local wellness gym down the street, and he takes and teaches swim classes.

There isn't a lot I can do around Ms. Nancy's house on my own, but I've insisted on doing our own laundry. I'm sure Ms. Nancy would prefer if I just put it all into the laundry bins with theirs. Instead, I wait until the machines are available. This doesn't always happen. Because Ms. Nancy enjoys doing laundry.

Every. Single. Day.

One practical reason is that Mr. Ray has dirty clothes daily (wet towels and shorts and T-shirts from the pool). But the other reason is that the woman can't sit still. As she'll tell you herself, she has to stay busy doing something, and laundry is one of those things. Even though I improved in a lot of areas when I went through the Proverbs 31 experiment, I know I still have a lot to learn when it comes to keeping house. I'm trying to see this time as an opportunity to learn from Ms. Nancy's ways and not gripe about them. Most of the time I do OK.

The hardest part for me is feeling forced to step back and have decisions made for me, or give up my preferences in respect to hers. For now this means using scent-free detergent and dryer sheets (we've always used the scented kind)—and definitely *no* fabric softener in the wash. This Downy girl is trying to get used to not-as-soft towels.

What this also means is I cook only when they're out of town. Because when I have offered to cook, usually what I suggest making isn't something they want to eat. So I don't offer to cook. Instead, I make sure I help keep the dishwasher loaded and unloaded, and the table cleaned off as soon as a meal is done. I understand their resistance. For most of our marriage, I wouldn't exactly have won any cooking awards. But I do think I've gotten better over the last two years. At least I'm not burning quesadillas anymore.

Working from the house is also a challenge. There are a lot of interruptions. I know it's just part of living in a house with so many different stages of life represented, but it's hard to get used to, especially since we've been by ourselves for so long. Family seems to come and go frequently, and it's a challenge to keep a routine, at least the way I've always been used to.

Now that Cliff is home and has a job, we're working hard to save so we can move into our own house. We've essentially started over. And we know we have a long way to go, but we're on our way to getting there. Yet at the moment, this house feels small. Very, very small.

Mr. Ray and Ms. Nancy both have their routines. She gets up before daylight, pours herself a cup of coffee, sits down in her favorite chair, and reads the paper she's walked out to the driveway in her robe to get. Then she answers the crossword puzzle in pencil. An hour or so later, Mr. Ray gets up, pours himself some coffee, and heads for the pool, which is less than a five-minute drive away.

It seems more often than not that the routines of our little family of three don't always happen in the larger scheme of things. I'll get Caleb up for school and to the kitchen for breakfast, and Papaw (as Mr. Ray is known to our ten-year-old) will tell him to go pick up his room. Or Nana (as Caleb calls Ms. Nancy) will ask him to bring her something before he does what I've just asked him to do. Or after school, I'll tell him to get started on his homework, and one of them will tell him to take out the trash. If I get confused and frustrated, I can't imagine how it feels for Caleb sometimes.

But I want to honor and respect my husband's parents. I want my son to respect and honor his grandparents. In an odd way, I feel like this is more training for the real work that will happen when it's just Cliff, Caleb, and me in our own home once again.

How did women do it when living with multiple generations was common? Did the daughters-in-law listen more to the mothers-in-law than to their husbands? Did the husbands listen more to their fathers (or, OK, maybe their mothers) than to their wives?

The kids in Caleb's group at church recently went to help at a local women's shelter in downtown Baton Rouge. I had a chance to talk to one of the social workers while we were there, and she shared that not all of the women living in the shelter were completely by themselves. Some did have parents or other family members living nearby. But those family members refused to help.

I'm sure there are extenuating circumstances in some of those cases. Maybe one too many bad choices had dried up all the goodwill. Or maybe the other family members just couldn't afford to help without putting themselves or their immediate families at financial risk. But the social worker said that some just didn't care enough. "You used to have families who helped each other out no matter what," she said. "That doesn't happen so much today."

I know we're blessed to have family that cares. I'm trying to remember that. Even when I'm waiting to do our laundry.

Where Does Submission Start?

I know this whole idea of submission isn't exactly on the priority list of most women. I don't think a lot of women these days wake up with the thought, *How can I help my husband today? How can I make sure I'm putting him first?* I think most of us assume we are putting our husbands first, or at least somewhat near the front, simply because of what we do.

I pick up his dry cleaning, right? I schedule his dentist appointments. Do I really have to actively think about helping him too? And letting him be "in charge"? Culture says we're crazy if we do. Or at the minimum, old-fashioned. Or maybe just odd. No, I think most of us who are wives and moms wake up thinking not about our husbands, but about The List. What we have to do. What we need to do. What we'd like to do, if everything else by some miracle gets done. We're juggling jobs and housework and home life and friends and family, not to mention all the extra activities our kids are involved in. Who really wants to worry about one more thing to check off the list, like submission?

This whole idea of submission doesn't really scream out "Winner" to me, anyway. Or "Trailblazer," for that matter. The very definition of the word means I'm yielding to something or someone else. I'm giving up my right (aren't I?), whatever that right is—whether it's my voice or my opinion or my will. After growing up listening to parents and teachers and youth pastors and Sunday school teachers tell me I can do and be whatever I want, the idea that now I'm supposed to willingly keep myself in second place simply because I walked down the aisle and said "I do" to someone else seems a little ridiculous.

Maybe this experiment is one silly idea. After all, Cliff doesn't care if I do this. He was just happy I've learned to cook a little more the last couple of years. I've taken some of the pressure off myself, and as a result, there seems to be a lot less pressure on our family. We're calmer. We're happier. Maybe I have already done enough. Why upset things now?

So this is where I'm stuck. During my last experiment, I learned that my goal, my focus, is not to be a superstar like the Proverbs 31 wife. My goal, my desire more than anything else is to be more like Jesus. My goal is to be the woman he wants me to be. And those instructions, those directions, come from God's Word.

The Bible seems to get such little respect today. There aren't just people around who don't believe it. They loudly don't believe it. They argue against it, actively question it, and seriously doubt it. Asking questions isn't a bad thing. We learn when we ask questions. I think the problem comes when we already assume we know the answers, and we throw the Bible's authority out completely and replace it with our own.

Today, it seems like even those of us who firmly plant ourselves within the church camp—folks who grew up with a spiritual footing—can fall into the trap of picking and choosing what we want from Scripture. We let Scripture support our already-formed opinions instead of allowing Scripture to form our opinions. But I don't believe that is God's intention.

Several verses in the Bible point to the importance of wives submitting to their husbands. Surely, they're in there for a reason. Not to be ignored, but applied. Like with a lot of Scripture, though, I think they've been misconstrued and misused and taken out of context for so long that it's much easier to ignore those verses or write them off. We cast them into the Old Testament bucket labeled "Historical Laws and Guidelines that Don't Really Apply Today" (even if a few of those Scriptures are listed in the New Testament). But I'm not so sure that's accurate.

I have to go back to what I've already learned about being a wife and mom. The Proverbs 31 experiment, if it taught me anything, showed me that bad things don't happen when you put someone else first. Great things happen when you put God first. A lot of good can come from putting others first. For starters, growth in yourself and your family. A deeper understanding of God and his desires for you.

And maybe that's where it starts. Maybe submission to our husbands first and foremost is submission to God. He's the one who created the relationship between man and woman to begin with, and he's the one who created marriage. (Yes, I know there are critics out there who say marriage is just a man-made institution. I respectfully disagree.) God had an original design and an original plan for marriage. One man. One woman. It cannot be mere coincidence that each gender has qualities the other doesn't, as much as our postmodern, gender-neutral-wishing culture might try to deflect.

Yet can we really say we submit to God's authority if we ignore what he's described in Scripture as the relationship between a husband and wife? Can we really just wing it and decide for ourselves how we believe it needs to be? Can we ignore what Scripture says or spend our time picking and choosing, as though it's some à la carte menu of our own making?

So what does the Bible say about submission?

Let's start with what Paul writes in Ephesians, beginning in verse 22:

> Wives, submit to your own husbands as to the Lord, for the husband is the head of the wife as Christ is the head of the church. He is the Savior of the body. Now as the church submits to Christ, so wives are to submit to their husbands in everything (Ephesians 5:22-24).

I like how The Message translation puts it: "Wives, understand and support your husbands in ways that show your support for Christ."

The same declaration is given in Colossians: "Wives, submit to your husbands, as is fitting for those who belong to the Lord" (Colossians 3:18 NLT).

Two years ago I might have read these words and ignored them. Submit to my husband in everything? Doesn't that just mean give up? Not have an identity? Am I just supposed to say no to myself and become some weird, domestic, modern version of a slave? What kind of marriage is that? What kind of life is that? No thank you.

But I need to dig deeper into this. I need to understand. So I checked out what the Greek word translated "submit" means. The word is *hupotassō*, which means to place or rank under. It means to subject oneself to another, to obey. Thoughts of getting whacked with a rolled up newspaper suddenly enter my mind. Not a comforting thought.

So I keep going. Some quick research tells me that *hupotassō* is in the form of what's called "middle voice," which doesn't really have an equivalent in English. Basically, it's not in either passive or active voice as it's more of a state of being. The subject of the text is entering the state or condition or action by her own initiative, or in response to something else. It's similar to what we might refer to as reflexive in English—she's acting or doing the action upon herself. As a wife, this isn't something that is done or something that needs to be done, but an ongoing choice.

I believe there's a reason God wants us to submit to our husbands. I just wish there was a clear list of what that does and doesn't look like. (I find it funny that during the Proverbs 31 experiment, I resented the fact there was a list on how to be a great wife, and here, in this context, I wish it was spelled out more clearly.)

But this whole idea of catering to a man, even if it's my husband, isn't popular in our culture. You won't find a woman, even in your small group at church, talking about all the ways she was happy to submit to her husband this week.

I think this has a lot to do with our attitudes as women toward men generally, and maybe more specifically in the workplace. Though I'm focusing on the relationship between a wife and her husband, still, the attitudes and the cultural mores we live with do have an effect on us. We're reminded that women make less than men for doing the same or even more work. We see it pointed out when women aren't included on a committee or in the president's cabinet or the CEO's board. We read articles on how to get ahead in a man's world and compete with men for that promotion while still maintaining our feminine mystique.

Here is what's eating at me. Here's the thought that's chipping away at the strong and independent womanly exterior I've built and maintained for so long—the version I created that I thought was comparable to men.

Maybe we're really not supposed to be just like men.

Is it such a far-out, crazy notion to think that we as women have our own special qualities that are enough to live up to without feeling this constant competition to one-up the male version of our species?

When I walked through my year's attempt to apply Proverbs 31 principles, I saw and discovered differences in myself that stood out from my husband. I am better at organizing. I am better at multitasking. And as much as I hate to say it, I really can do a better job than Cliff at cleaning the toilet. (Read *My So-Called Life as a Proverbs 31 Wife* to understand that one.) Many studies show that the brains of men and women are hard-wired differently. Men don't see some of the things we see. They don't consider some (OK, maybe many) of the things we can consider when it comes to an issue or a topic or a scenario. They're more simple. We're more complex. Wow, are we complex.

So why again do we have to be just like the guys?

Why is it so important we have as many women as men CEOs, as evidenced by the articles every year that decry the fact we don't? Who decided that where you sit in the conference room is the real measurement of success for a woman and that the home is a pathetic platform to point to for feelings of worth and satisfaction? Why are there so many special awards given to women for being successful *as* women in career and industry if women just want to be equal counterparts to men? Because if that's what we want, then why do we complain that many workplaces and industries aren't sensitive to women's needs as wives and moms and recognize the companies and corporations that are?

What in the world do we as women want? I'm sure men don't know. But I'm not sure women do, either. Because if I'm feeling a little confused at the moment, I have a feeling other women are too.

But maybe, just maybe before any of these questions are asked, the first question should be, what does God want? What does God want for me as a woman? What does God want for me as a wife?

Maybe that's where I have to start. Because for a long time, if I'm very honest, I've ignored that last part. I don't look at myself as a woman or a wife. I'm an individual. I'm a person.

Why do I do that?

Why can't I embrace that God made me a woman and there are traits in women that can't be found in men, and it is very good? Maybe I should also consider another note from my Bible concordance: that there is a reason for the order in which the genders were created. There is a meaning behind it. There is a purpose. God didn't save the best for last by creating Eve after Adam, as I've heard many women joke. Genesis 2:20 tells us God created Eve to help Adam, and she was unique in her qualities and unique in her role. He didn't create her to be a slave to Adam but to assist him, to support him, to come to his aide. To provide companionship so he wouldn't be lonely. God created her to live in harmony together with Adam in the land God created.

But God didn't create Eve first. He didn't create Eve to run the show. He created her to be a complement. Some translations say a helper. One version says companion.

Complement means "to complete." I saw this meaning lived out during my experiment and the time I put in as a wife and mom during the whole Proverbs 31 thing. Something clicked when I began accepting the whole idea of being a thermostat for my family and that my actions had a huge influence on the temperament in our household.

I don't think it has to do with personality, either. Cliff is mild-mannered and gentle. I'm definitely more assertive and take-charge. But if opposites attract and work together, that wasn't necessarily the case for us. There was a lot of friction in our earlier years of marriage. I tried to lead, he often followed, and we still argued and fussed. It was only after I started attempting to follow some of the Proverbs 31 qualities, less in charge and more of a helper, that we noticed more peace in our home.

Is it possible submission can bring peace too? That's a little harder to wrap my brain around.

Mamaw Moves In

"Sara, I need your help."

It was Ms. Nancy and she'd called me from the road. Something in her voice sounded urgent.

"Ray's mom is coming to live with us."

As she threw out a list of things she needed me to complete, mainly preparing Mamaw's room while she and Mr. Ray drove over to Texas to get her, I felt the color drain from my face. There was some serious change about to happen in the Horn house. I was getting tired of change. What in the world was God thinking?

I thought about everything we already had going on. I was helping our church out by coaching kindergarten cheerleaders for Upward Basketball. Cliff was coaching one of the basketball teams and Caleb was playing on one. I was about to start my first online graduate class. And subbing at the nearby elementary school as much as I could.

I wanted to be helpful. I knew Ms. Nancy couldn't possibly be looking forward to this any more than I could. She was already making space for a daughter-in-law; now she was making space for a mother-in-law too—one she didn't always get along with (or maybe who didn't always get along with *her).*

But Mamaw wasn't feeling good. Her stomach hurt and she'd stopped eating. And in her nineties, living with a sister about her age, she didn't have anyone really able to look out for her. Mr. Ray and Ms. Nancy were the dependable ones Mamaw counted on when the going got tough. Now she was counting on them to move her in with them.

And us. What was now three generations under one roof was about to become four.

And our small guest bathroom was about to get even smaller. And probably smellier. Like old-people smellier.

Not that there's anything wrong with old-people smells. I'm sure I will in fact smell like old people one day. In thirty, forty, fifty years.

Oh. Dear. Lord.

Even as I assured Ms. Nancy I'd take care of what she'd asked me to do—washing sheets, emptying a dresser, making room in a closet—my frustration was growing. No one had asked if we were OK with this. I felt selfish for even thinking the thought, but wasn't there enough already happening in this house that we didn't have to bring more into it?

But I already knew my mother-in-law's stance on this subject. You helped family. No matter what. I, after all, was a beneficiary of that philosophy. So was Cliff. So was Caleb. I was really, really trying to learn the lesson. And apparently God wanted me to learn this lesson too.

Now I needed to let Cliff know. He was at work when he picked up the phone.

"Uh, what?" he said.

I explained what had just happened.

"For how long?" he asked.

I told him I had no idea, but that it sounded pretty open-ended. Ms. Nancy wasn't sure.

I heard a loud sigh that totally reflected what I was already feeling. These walls were already closing in. I tried to ignore the stupid tears forming at the corners of my eyes.

"What are we going to do?" I asked.

Our answer came that night right after we got Caleb to bed. You never saw two people jump online to look at houses so fast.

Mamaw's move into the house with us was actually pretty uneventful. For one thing, she didn't bring a whole lot with her. Some clothes, her Bible, a few pictures. Her medicine. A cell phone that kept her connected to everyone in her life who really mattered to her. Her sister and her sister's daughter promised to send the rest of her clothes in a box the following week.

Despite being ninety-two, Mamaw still moves around pretty well. She speaks slowly, in her long Mississippi drawl, and likes to pepper her conversation with a lot of "Weeeellll" and "Aaaany ways…" as she tells her stories, many we've heard often. She reminds me of a bird, both in her face and her stature. A very tough bird. She's weathered quite a few storms in her day and hasn't yet let one knock her completely down. Though she wasn't feeling very good, she still seemed to be doing OK. I wondered if it was more a feeling of loneliness than anything else.

I wasn't stressing anymore about her moving in with us. After Ms. Nancy's call that first day, and I'd had a chance that night for my little pity party, I got over it. When Mamaw walked through the door a few days later, I greeted her with a big smile and a hug.

Change is like that sometimes for me. I panic with the initial shock of it all, and then I take a deep breath, accept it, regroup, and move on. In some ways, I thought it was a blessing to have Mamaw with us. I was never close to either of my parents' parents.

Growing up, my family always lived away from my parents' extended families—my dad's side on the West coast and my mom's on the East. There was usually drama and tension on my mom's side, and though unintentional, indifference and a lack of communication on my father's side. (Remember how I said my dad is pretty quiet? It was a genetic trait.) My parents didn't do much with either of their families, and I grew up without a lot of connection to our family tree, or really any idea of what it meant to be close to grandparents.

My dad's mother passed away when he was twenty, and I'd seen his dad exactly twice in my lifetime. I don't think it was that he couldn't afford the flight from California out to wherever we lived; I just think it wasn't really ever a priority. My mom called him more than my dad did to say hi and keep what connection she could. Just two years after Cliff and I married, my grandfather passed away, and I remember sitting on the floor in our bedroom, sobbing hard on Cliff's shoulder. I didn't cry because I would miss my grandfather but because I'd never known him. The loss felt surprisingly deep, like an empty hole I knew would never be filled.

Grandmother, Ms. Nancy's mother, was the first grandparent I ever personally knew, at least consistently. Toward the end of her life, she came to live with the Horns shortly after Cliff and I first married. They'd fixed up the pool house behind their home at the time into a converted apartment so she and Edna Earl had their own space. Bound to a wheelchair, Grandmother kept herself busy quilting and dipping snuff (something she'd done since she was eight years old), and during those years we lived nearby, I'd enjoyed getting to spend time with her before she finally passed away.

I always looked forward to hearing her greet me with "Come 'n 'ere!" when she spied me through the screen door. She often sat in her wheelchair by her quilting table in front of the window and the sunshine. She was a special lady. We were living in Tennessee finishing up our degrees when she finally passed away, but we got to say good-bye at Christmas, just a month or so before her funeral.

Ms. Nancy cared for her mom the last three years of her life, with some help from her sister, and had done everything for Grandmother. Now she was being asked to help her husband's mother. She'd done what she could to ensure Mamaw's extended visit would be comfortable for her. She'd put new sheets and bedspread on the twin bed we'd placed in the room. She'd cleaned out as much of the closet as she could. She'd hung pretty new curtains on the windows.

After some of the aggravation and pressure I'd started feeling myself the last couple of months, more from me being ready for our own space than anything else, I realized it might be a little fun to watch my mother-in-law have to deal with *her* mother-in-law. Especially since Mamaw's choice of chore around the house seemed to be the laundry too.

Seriously. What is it about women and laundry?

It's hard to think about submission to my husband at the moment when everything feels as if it's out of my control. But I know family is important to Cliff and so it needs to be important to me. That's a start, right?

Sex Before Breakfast

This weekend I flew to Asheville, NC, and served as part of the staff for a marriage conference for military couples that Billy Graham's ministry offers twice a year. I was excited to teach a workshop on what it means to rely on God's strength for our lives as military wives, but I was also a little sad Cliff couldn't come with me. His drill weekend was the same weekend, which happens more often than not. Caleb got to hang out with his grandparents and Cliff planned on picking me up at the airport on his way back from drill Sunday night.

While every marriage has challenges, military marriages come with their own unique set. I know wives who have been married to their husbands longer than they've actually lived together thanks to trainings and deployments. Maintaining close intimacy can be hard for a couple when one spouse is on the other side of the world for so much of the time. And even after the spouse comes home, lots of issues often have to be worked through. It takes time to grow back together, and it's hard sometimes to find common ground. Especially when in the back of your mind, you know they'll be leaving again.

The main speaker for the weekend spent much of his time in the main sessions unpacking the story of creation and Adam and Eve.

We read in Genesis about the world God creates. Everything is beautiful—beautiful garden, beautiful animals, plants, trees, and God then creates Adam to be part of his world. After seeing Adam's need for companionship, God also creates Eve to be—as I mentioned earlier—Adam's helper.

Everything is beautiful and wonderful until sin enters the picture. God gives Adam and Eve only one rule—"you must not eat from the tree of the knowledge of good and evil"—and Eve, after listening to Satan himself in the guise of a snake, chooses not to listen. Then she influences her husband to do the same, and he makes the same choice.

I listened closely to the speaker's words. "Don't let the world teach you theology," he said, over and over. I think there's a lot of truth to that.

When we look at Adam and Eve's story and their life together, we can see God had a design in mind. He had a plan and a purpose for each of them—he had a reason for the man and he had a reason for the woman. There was promise for each. God saw how each was intended to be. But in our culture, we've convoluted and added chaos to what was supposed to be pretty straightforward.

I'm not interested in going back to the days where women had no vote or really any voice. I don't think God intended that in his original plan. We can look to many strong women with confident voices in the Bible as examples: Deborah, who served as a judge and stepped in when an army commander failed to follow God's direction (Judges 5); Miriam, the sister of Moses, who not only played a crucial role in God's plan to place her brother in the midst of Egypt royalty to one day set his people free, but also helped lead them (Exodus 15:20); Phoebe and Priscilla, who both played active leadership roles in their respective churches, considered by Paul to be coworkers in ministry (Romans 16).

But when I listen to the voices of women today, there's a lot of clamoring to be first, to be on top. I have been that woman. I have sat in the conference room, trying to stake my claim on top of the corporate mountain. I've sat at my desk and tried not to be annoyed at male coworkers coming back from running with the boss during their lunch hour, knowing they've talked about work projects for which I would also have loved to have offered input.

But what if there were a different way? What if there has been a different way and we've just missed it? Missed it because of what our mothers in the sixties and seventies did? Buy into this "be all you can be" as women—a great concept, but one in which maybe we moved down a slightly wrong path?

Earlier this month I spoke to a book club of older women (mostly retirees and grandmothers) and when I shared that I was about to start this project of learning what it means to be a submissive wife, you could have heard a pin drop. No one even smiled. I expect most women to at least chuckle when I tell them what I'm doing, because I know it sounds so crazy. This sweet group of ladies could barely breathe (though I'm sure they all agreed that I was crazy).

But what if we have missed it?

When I was in my early twenties and early in my marriage and deep into career objectives and goal-planning and figuring out exactly what I needed to do to get to where I wanted to be, a dangerous question sometimes hovered at the back of my mind and nagged at me like a mosquito that wouldn't leave the room. There were days I glanced over at my sweet, laid-back husband—the guy who sometimes needs to be reminded to take the trash out, who still can't balance a checkbook, and who might be perfectly happy living on Ramen noodles if I weren't around to help plan meals—and that quiet whisper would ask, *Do I really need him anyway?* And there were times—in my complaining, during our heated arguments, in the middle of total marital frustration, both of us on opposite sides of the room, leaned against the walls like boxers in a ring—when Cliff asked me the same question: "Do you really even need me?"

Seriously.

What an awful, horrible thought. Yet, I don't think it's too far a stretch to say there are women today who have that same thought. In moments of frustration. At times when hurtful words are blurted out without thinking. During selfish misunderstandings and misguided attempts for clarity. And while it may not be the convincer or reason for so many marriages that end today, it's a starting gun that leads to attitudes that can lead to those unhappy endings.

The truth is I do need my husband. I know, today, I need him. God put him in my life because I need him. Not just because I want him. In God's plan for me, my Creator, the One who knew me before I was born, who knew I would be here on this earth he also created, he knew I needed Cliff. And Cliff needed me. And when we convince ourselves otherwise, we're the ones making an awful, horrible mistake.

We can't let the world teach us theology.

For years I have followed what other people say about marriage. That it's a two-way street, that it's fifty-fifty, that marriage is a partnership that only works when both partners work together. But when I pick up God's Word, when I read what the Bible says about wives and husbands and the specific roles they have, I'm convicted and reminded again that this Book, this collection of pages that so many scoff at and want to forget about today—that this Book is holy. That marriage is holy and sacred and it's a gift. It's a precious treasure. But we're being taught, we're allowing ourselves to be led, by a culture that doesn't even know God nor respect him, and we're being convinced over time that marriage isn't special. It's really just an old-fashioned institution that isn't necessary today. The commitment we make when we say our vows in front of God and witnesses comes with conditions we add of our own choosing, and when those conditions break, we can leave. The commitment, like a breached contract, doesn't count anymore.

I'm not sure what biblical submission completely looks like just yet. I don't know if it means I have to follow my husband around like a pet poodle, catering to his every whim, or that I simply stand with him, both of us heroes on the same team, striving to follow God together. But I know this. I want to apply what the Bible says. Not what others say. Because if there's one thing I know, it's that the world does a lousy job interpreting theology.

She hung around after my workshop, waiting for me to finish talking with some other wives. She was quiet, but I could tell by her eyes she had a question. One that was pretty serious.

As the room emptied out, she introduced herself. Like most of the women there that weekend, Lucy (not her real name) was an army wife. She and her husband had been married less than a year, and she had a son who was seven from a previous relationship. They were young, and even though they should have still been in their honeymoon phase, they were already having problems.

She hesitantly began to explain. Her relationship with her husband was teetering and she wasn't sure they would make it. We sat down and I asked her what bothered her so much about her marriage.

"He always wants to have sex!" she whispered, rolling her eyes and clutching her hands. OK, I wasn't expecting that. She explained how it seemed her husband's desire for sex and her desire for sex were on completely different ends of the spectrum. More like two ends of the Grand Canyon. He wanted it more often, and way more than she wanted it.

"And he wants it in the mornings, like right after we wake up," she told me. "Which is just ridiculous! I have stuff to do, I have to get my son up and ready for school. Who has time for sex before breakfast? Who really *wants* sex before breakfast?"

I could understand where she was coming from. When I wake up, my thoughts usually go right to my day and what I have to get done. Cuddling is nice and all, but when you've got a clock running in the back of your brain, it's a little more difficult to be in the mood. For Lucy, though, it was really hard. She wasn't a morning person, and it was hard enough for her to get up and take care of her son. But to also try and be romantic with her husband? Before she'd even brushed her teeth or taken a shower? This was leading to frequent arguments and hurt feelings, and her husband had finally thrown down the big word.

Submission. As in, "The Bible says you have to submit to me, so when I want sex, you have to do it."

Oh no, please tell me he didn't. Because that's the way to make your wife want to love you—as she walks out the door.

I got a little more serious and asked her a few more questions. I wanted to make sure this wasn't a case of abuse. It wasn't. Just a case of a seriously testosterone-induced male wanting some time with his honey. And the more she refused, the more he insisted and the more she balked. And nobody was getting any—uh, peace and happiness.

In their marriage, sex had become a battleground, a stake in a bigger war neither one was going to win.

Lucy wanted to know what I thought and what she should do. Mainly, how she could get her husband to leave her alone. And quit with the submission thing already.

Silently, I prayed for words of wisdom. And I thought about my own marriage.

Ten years earlier, I probably could have sat exactly where Lucy was right now. I enjoyed sex, but maybe like a lot of women, it wasn't always as much a priority for me as it was for my sweet husband. There were times I'd looked at it more as a duty than a joy, something else to check off because I was so focused on other things. Over time, though, God helped me see how wrong that attitude was. He'd taught me that spending those intimate hours with my husband wasn't just about fulfilling a need or a physical desire, but it was also an important part of communicating in our relationship. It was a time we could grow closer together.

I smiled at Lucy. "I think that both of you may be looking at this wrong." She was looking at this as a control thing. I couldn't say for sure but maybe her husband was too. Or maybe he was looking at it as a way to connect, and when she refused, then it became a control thing for him as well. If anything, sex between them had become a selfish thing. What he wanted versus what she wanted.

The story of a lot of marriages.

Couples argue about a lot of things. Sex shouldn't be one of them. Sex should bring couples together. It should be the most intimate act of love and trust that a marriage can have.

But sex in a marriage often gets used as a power play. She uses it to get what she wants, like a yes to a new couch or a new car. He uses it, well, because he wants it. But I don't believe God intended it to be used that way.

In 1 Corinthians 7:2-5, we're told that both the husband and wife should fulfill each other's sexual needs. I like how The Message translation words it: "The marriage bed must be a place of mutuality—the husband seeking to satisfy his wife, the wife seeking to satisfy her husband. Marriage is not a place to 'stand up for your rights.' Marriage is a decision to serve the other, whether in bed or out."

Based on what God's Word says, sex between a husband and a wife should be good. Loving. Intimate. Never used for manipulation. Using sex to get our way or to punish our spouse for doing or not doing something we wanted is not how God wants it used. I think as women, we sometimes get so focused on the physical part of sex that we totally miss the emotional reasons we have this act of passion in our marriages.

For me, sex with my husband is our purest and closest form of intimacy as two people who have committed our lives to each other. I'm afraid that the passion behind sex has become watered down and, in some cases, seen as meaningless. With so many, even Christians, giving themselves permission to think it's OK to have sex before marriage, is it any wonder the act of sex itself is seen as less special? Maybe not so important? The bond of marriage—sure, maybe that still has some meaning, but let's not bring sex into it, right?

My husband and I are blessed to be each other's first and only. I don't say that lightly. With an engagement of over eighteen months, there were plenty of moments we thought about not waiting. But our desire to follow

God's design for sex outweighed our desire for each other until our wedding night, and we were so grateful we did wait.

As Lucy and I talked, I shared that one thing I have learned over the years is that men communicate differently than we do as women and that quite often, when we're responsive to them, they're more responsive to us. I'm not sure that's what she wanted to hear, but as I explained, sometimes it requires one person to take the first step toward thinking of the other person.

I suggested she talk to her husband at a time when they were both in good moods, not first thing in the morning, and explain to him her stress about getting up in the mornings to take care of her son, but also to let him know she still enjoyed being with him. And maybe give it a try at least once. There's nothing wrong with a little variety once in a while, right?

My First, Oh-So-Not-Submissive Mistake

I got home with a lot still to think about when it comes to submission. But I had other things needing my focus too.

We're ready for our own place. And as nice as it's been living with family, I'm thinking it will be just as nice to come for visits.

But there's a problem.

The well is dry.

While Cliff was deployed last year, I worked hard to save as much of what he made as possible. When we lived in South Carolina, my job covered our bills, and I put a lot of his earnings away in the bank for safekeeping. But in the six months he was home and looking for full-time work, we still had to pay our bills (which in the grand scope of things was minimal), and we were still paying Cliff's parents rent each month.

While he was away, we'd agreed I wouldn't accept speaking opportunities so I could stay focused on Caleb and his needs. And though I'd finished up two books while he was gone, and freelanced a little after we'd moved back to live with the Horns, I'd kept that agreement. The whole Proverbs 31 experiment gave me so much to think about, in many ways, I used that time before Cliff got home to still process all I'd learned. I enjoyed helping Caleb get comfortable in his new surroundings and his new school as we both adjusted to being back with family and, at least for me, old friends.

But with no regular income for either of us and expenses still going out, our savings dried up. And now the prospect of moving into our home with a nice little down payment, as we'd dreamed, looks pretty bleak.

We were relieved when Cliff was hired to work for the state after five months of looking. Now, at least, we're no longer staring at a completely unanswerable question of whether we will be able to move—we're just trying to figure out when.

We're trying not to rush it. We're trying to be smart.

But it isn't easy. For one thing, I'm not sure my mother-in-law sees what I do as a real job. She's not alone—most people have difficulty seeing folks who spend their days writing, as actually doing work. She seems more excited for me when I'm out of the house working as a substitute at Caleb's school than when I'm sitting at my desk at home, tapping away on my laptop. And though I know Cliff approves and supports what I do and understands the responsibilities I have with the military wives ministry I run along with everything else I'm doing, still, I feel the silent pressure. And right or wrong, I want her approval. And I worry I'm not doing enough and that I need to do more. Much, much more.

Now that Mamaw has moved in, a few things have changed that elevate that feeling. We've lost the office setup we had. That room became Mamaw's bedroom, so Ms. Nancy's desk went to her bedroom. My desk went into the living room. As in the central area of the house where everyone—and all visitors—congregate. Now after I drop Caleb off at school in the mornings, I sit at my desk to write or to work on an assignment for one of the graduate classes I've started, and I listen to Mamaw and Mr. Ray as they sit on the sofas two feet away and talk about the day's weather. And if it will rain by afternoon. And what they ate for breakfast. And what they'll have for lunch. What doctor visits they have coming up. And in the afternoons, they talk about their naps they had earlier.

And I listen to this. Every single day.

I've finally resorted to wearing headphones so I don't constantly feel like I'm living in a retirement village. If they break out the Bingo set, I know I'm in trouble.

I try not to say much to Cliff. He's only in his third month of his new job, and I'm trying to help him stay focused as he settles into his position. I want to be his helper. He's working as a public information officer helping public school teachers figure out their retirement benefits. Not as glamorous as the marketing job he once had for the Christian radio station in Nashville, but it's a paycheck. We're grateful.

Still, state jobs don't pay much, and if we're ever going to move into our own place, we need to find some new sources of income.

That's when I saw it. Our local weekly paper listed a position on their Facebook page for a part-time editorial assistant. Surely I could do that job with ease. And it was part-time, so I could still do the other things I needed to, including my graduate classes. I wasn't sure how much the job paid, but it was worth checking out. And at least I could show Ms. Nancy I was trying.

I quickly updated my résumé, wrote up a friendly cover letter, and emailed everything over to the editor. By that afternoon, I'd talked with her on the phone, and we tentatively planned to talk again in a couple of days.

When Ms. Nancy got home from running errands, I proudly told her what I'd just done and got her full approval.

"I saw that and was going to mention it to you," she said. "It looks like the perfect job for you."

I eagerly agreed with her, happy she approved. Things were looking up.

There was only one small problem.

I forgot to ask Cliff.

※

Small-town living has its advantages. For one thing, you usually know a lot more people than you might living in a big city. More folks are willing to help when you need it, or offer an encouraging word when you're not even looking for it. But small-town living also has its disadvantages. For one thing, there are a lot of people around you who think they already know you.

Most folks around here remember me as the little ten-year-old who could sing, the one who stood up on the First Baptist Church stage in pigtails and glasses and a red, white, and blue dress one Fourth of July and belted out "The Fifty States that Rhyme," in double time no less. They remember our wedding one hot, sticky Saturday in June. We were the first wedding to hold a reception in the church atrium, a space the church had just completed, and my mother and I thought it would be perfect, especially when it came time to throw the bouquet off one of the tall, elegant staircases.

Our wedding was also the first to almost catch the sanctuary on fire. After the ceremony was over, everyone headed toward the reception line in the atrium. Someone forgot to blow out the candles on the platform, and a rogue fake flower blossom was too close to the flame. Eventually, it dropped to the tile floor below, smoldering and filling up the entire space with white smoke and forcing the wedding party to delay pictures until the haze lifted. Yes, we are also why the church now has a no-drip candle policy.

Eighteen months later we moved away to Tennessee to finish school. That was about the same time my parents separated. Just a few years earlier, I'd thrown them a big twenty-fifth wedding anniversary party, where they'd renewed their vows. I'd collected and arranged a huge scrapbook of letters from their friends all around the country who wished them the best and another twenty-five years together. But watching them that evening repeat the lines they'd said when they first began made me more sad and wistful than happy and hopeful. In hindsight, that vow renewal had served as a last grasp at a relationship that had already decayed from solid into vapor. By the time Caleb came along, their marriage was over and the divorce was pending. I really never had any intention of moving back to this town. The pain, for a long time, outweighed the joy.

But I'm thankful that hearts have a way of healing over time, and more than ten years have passed. I think I've reached a place where I can see our little family of three making a fresh start here. There's security in the familiarity of one's roots. And of all the places my parents moved us, this town offers the closest thing to roots I've ever known.

So, it's partly from wanting to feel a stronger connection to those roots that I think it may be a good idea to work for the town's weekly paper. And it would provide the extra income we're looking for.

But Cliff wasn't so sure.

I realized my mistake the moment I opened my mouth.

"Hey, so I have that job interview this afternoon!"

I'd called him at the office to tell him. But Cliff was quiet. And not nearly as excited as I was.

"O…K," he said. "When did this happen?"

That's when it hit me. Um, submissive wives don't go all let-me-go-apply-for-a-job without first talking to the husband. Clearly, I needed a better manual for this whole thing. Or maybe I should follow the one I already have. (You know, the Bible.) Copying down Scripture and gluing it to my hands might be a good idea. (Didn't they do something like that in the Old Testament?)

"It's part-time, twenty-five hours a week," I said, "but it will fit in with Caleb's school so I won't be working when he's home and it's extra money and I think I have a really good shot at getting it!"

"Yeah, but when are you going to work on your book?" my wise husband asked. "What about your grad classes? That's a whole lot of stuff to work on, and you've just shortened your time by half."

"OK, so what do you want me to do? I thought we needed extra money. I'm trying to help. I'm trying to do my part."

"I know and I appreciate that, but you're already doing your part by what you do with Caleb and what you're doing with your writing and your speaking."

I knew he had a point. But I also knew I was going to go crazy if we didn't get our own place soon. A house still seemed like the best option. Monthly rent in town for an apartment was way more than a monthly payment for a mortgage would be. I'd checked.

"OK, so do you want me to cancel the interview?" I said, trying to sound respectful and not frustrated.

"No, go ahead and do the interview," he said, sounding more resigned than I wanted him to. "I just want you to be sure you can handle all of it."

"I think I can."

I really hoped I could, anyway.

I made it through my interviews with Sheila just fine. The first one was by phone where she'd reviewed my résumé and the second one was with her in the office. The newspaper had just moved into a space at the end of a short strip mall, and she'd proudly showed me the awards the paper had received since she'd been there as editor for the last five years.

I knew my mother-in-law's opinion about the paper and how often she'd sat at her desk at the travel agency over the years, correcting typos and grammatical errors with each issue, so I wasn't completely impressed. But maybe that was before Sheila had started working there. I wasn't completely sure what it would be like working for her. My optimistic self had the unfortunate habit of always seeing the best in every situation until it was too late to get out of it.

Sheila's biggest concern was that I was overqualified to be an assistant, considering my writing and web experience. I was ready for that argument. I told her I wasn't looking for a manager role. I'd done that, and I was focused on other things. I was really just looking for a role where I could be a support and something that would fit with my life as a wife and mom. I tried not to talk about my books or the online graduate classes I'd just started.

She called the next day and offered me the position, which I gladly accepted. I beat out a college student with no experience and a housewife who was looking for something to keep her less bored. Managing the news content for the website would be my main responsibility, and I could write and edit as needed.

I was excited and felt like I was doing what our family needed, and maybe also what was expected by other members of the family. Still, I couldn't help but feel a little twinge of something at the edges of my heart. Had I rushed into this? Was I ignoring this whole submission thing before I really even got started?

I'm not sure what I expected working for a community paper. But I immediately thought about what my husband likes to say about his days working for his high-school paper—it's not really about all the news that's fit to print but what news actually fits in print. Specifically around ads. I understand ads pay for papers, but stories should also inspire readers to want to read it and subscribe. And there seemed to be a tension between the two, at least between the editorial side of things (Sheila and me) and the advertising side.

I've tried to stay open-minded, but it's not easy. One afternoon, Sheila pulled up a chair next to me in my small space of a cubicle and offered to walk me through the *AP Style Guide*. As we squeezed together, looking over some notes she'd brought with her, I tried not to think that I'd just been put in Remedial Journalism 101. *It's always good to review what you know*, I told myself, and I tried to keep a patient and professional attitude as she took me through her proofreading quiz, a sample paragraph with a lot of errors and a few examples of style issues. We reviewed the paragraph one word at a time, and she asked what I'd change. Some things were specific. Other things subjective, based on personal preference and style. I did pretty well but missed something minor. Laughing at myself, I told Sheila I was sorry.

"I guess I've spent more time on *Chicago Style* the last few years," I said, giving her a smile.

"What's that?" she said. "I've never heard of that."

I paused and took a breath.

"Oh, um, it's just the style guide a lot of book publishers and magazines use instead of *AP*," I said. I really wanted to change the subject. One, so I didn't run the risk of making my new boss feel or look bad, and two, so I could distract myself from the little voice in the back of my head whispering, *What have you gotten yourself into?*

There are benefits. My schedule is flexible and fits perfectly with Caleb's school hours. I drop him off in the morning, drive to the office, and leave when it's time to pick him up from school. The best part is that office, school, and house are all three minutes or less apart. And this is a job that stays at the office, which I could never have said when I worked full-time for my previous employers. It's a good thing, too, because I don't have a lot of time to think about work at the newspaper when I get home.

I've officially started my master's degree in Christian leadership. I'm not sure I'm ready, to be honest. And this may have been the worst possible time to start it. But I did it with Cliff's blessing and part of his GI Bill, though I don't know if even he had an idea of what the commitment would require. In order to qualify for the scholarship our church offered, I had to take three classes this semester. Two during the first half, one in the last. And I haven't studied anything in the last seven or eight years.

It's a challenge, but I've figured out a routine. I pick Caleb up from school, we get home, and he has a snack of cheese and summer sausage or chips and salsa or whatever other goodies his Nana has brought home for him and the other grandsons when they come over. Once he's settled working on his homework, I grab a textbook and take off for our room, sitting on the bed with pillows stacked behind me. There are hundreds of pages to read each week, with discussion questions to answer and online tests to get ready for. The nerd in me is excited for the challenge to crack open the books again—but the kid inside with serious ADD issues is not feeling so confident. I wonder how I can concentrate effectively when so many other things are going on.

I'm only in my second week at the paper, but it is becoming much more than I expected it to be. The job doesn't feel part-time; I'm there from 8:30 in the morning till I leave at 3:00, Monday through Friday. Sheila keeps offering to increase my hours if I'd like, but that is the last thing I want, and I'm trying to resist as politely as I can. Which, thinking about it, is a first for me—I used to thrive on working more than required. Following my sophomore year in college, I took a break and came home and got a job at the local Christian radio station. After I'd been on the job just a few months, my supervisor came back from vacation to find my two-week timesheet clocking in at an impressive ninety hours. With a seriously perturbed look on his face, he had to explain to me, his eager and enthusiastic nineteen-year-old employee, what budgets were.

The folks at the newspaper are an interesting group. There are a couple of salespeople, a designer, a couple of support staff, Sheila (the editor who also serves as reporter, photographer, and whatever else is needed to get the paper out each week), and Larry, the managing editor and publisher. Larry comes and goes a few times a week since the company who owns this paper also owns several others in surrounding towns and parishes. He has a large office with floor-to-ceiling doors that also serves as the conference room, and then the rest of the space consists of one long narrow room that runs from the front entrance area all the way to the very back. Cubbies for salespeople and for me run along the right side of the room, with small offices for the office manager, advertising manager, and Sheila on the opposite wall.

My goal is to be open to whatever situations God puts in front of me, but I'm struggling a bit as I've settled into working here. Smoke breaks happen two to three times a day, out the back door of the building, which happens to be three feet from my desk, and several troop out there like clockwork to get their fix. I'm learning to live without breathing much, at least through my nose anyway.

I'm also trying to learn how to audibly edit out the swearing that goes on in regular conversation. The long open room, even with its cubby dividers, carries voices from one end to the other, and it's hard to not hear what people are saying, whether they're on the phone or talking to each other. It seems silly to me why people have to cuss, especially in a professional work environment. Doing it when you're truly ticked off and just don't know any better is one thing, I guess, but it seems so pointless to use those words like any other adjective or adverb in your vocabulary. I try to keep my face to the computer screen, do my job, and leave the job behind when I head home. I want to do my best—but I also want to avoid getting so caught up with the job that I find myself doing the same thing I was doing before.

It took longer than I wish it had, but I learned from my Proverbs 31 experiment that I had to seriously examine my priorities and where I'd placed my family in that mix. My personal drive to make a difference and my affinity for accomplishment often put everything related to home and hearth on the back burner. I discovered I'd missed out on so many of the simple joys of being a mom and being a wife, viewing responsibilities that came with those roles as duties instead of privileges. But tackling this new experiment as a wife desiring to be submissive to my husband has made me realize I still have questions.

I'm still wrestling with the whole work and career question. When I was younger, certainly before I was married, and probably for the first ten years of my marriage, I never thought twice about working. I never questioned that I would work—I always knew I would. Not just for monetary reasons, but because I knew there was more to my life than raising babies and cleaning house all day. That's how I viewed it, anyway, in those early days. And my mother and every woman her age that I knew encouraged me to pursue my dreams—to get out there and go for it and let nothing hold me back.

My mother gave me only one word of warning before I got married about the challenge of being a wife and mom. At the time, I wanted to pursue a music career, and my mom told me I'd never be able to do that and still have a family too. That thought seemed so out of place from what I had been told all my life growing up—what I'd believed and what I'd worked toward—that I immediately put it out of my mind and didn't think any more about it. Until after I became a mom and I worked full time and I noticed I was failing miserably to keep career, house, and home all going at once. Then I started to get an inkling of what my mother was trying to help me understand and prepare for.

My experiment with the Proverbs 31 wife helped me see that life happens in seasons, but that not all seasons are equal. I began to realize dreams change with the days that pass and desires in one season no longer find the same spot on the priority shelf as another.

All of those realizations have helped. I've come to not just accept but embrace the roles God's given me as a wife and mom. I believe in the difference I make in keeping a beautiful home (even if that consists at the moment of only two bedrooms and a small guest bathroom) because it's no longer just a place where my family lives, but a place where my family is strengthened. I love spending time with my son because I know time is an investment in what he will do and who he will be as an adult with his own family. I see the beauty of Timothy and his mother and grandmother's time with him as we read about it in 2 Timothy 1:4-5, and I want to witness that in my son's life. I want to be that encouragement for him. I want to be an encouragement for my husband.

But I don't find anywhere in the Bible where it says a woman must stay home and do nothing else. And I wonder if that even makes sense for women today, especially in a struggling economy with so much financial uncertainty. Many women have to work, whether they want to or not. Even in the Proverbs 31 passage, this woman's aptitude for business and her enjoyment of work is pointed out multiple times. She's a businesswoman as much as she is a housewife.

What's best? What's blessed?

I go back and forth. And some days, I don't really know.

A Lesson in Submission

Mamaw has settled into the Horn household and seems to feel much better. It hasn't been easy for Ms. Nancy, though. Earlier this week, we had what will forever be known as "The Mamaw Laundry Room Incident."

I got up at my usual time, threw on some clothes, and stepped out of our room to feed our dog, Sammy. At five in the morning, even by my morning person standards, I'm not always thinking clearly, and I noticed in my bare feet, some water on the laundry room floor. I assumed Sammy or someone else had kicked his water bowl, and I went on with getting ready for my day, telling myself I'd go back and wipe it up after I did what I needed to.

After I got completely ready—shower, hair, makeup—I stepped out into the hall and noticed Ms. Nancy standing in the laundry room. She looked at me, just a couple of feet away, and since Mamaw's room was just to the right of the laundry room, she whispered to me, "It smells like *pee* in here."

I didn't remember smelling anything, but then again, my sinuses are clogged up most of the time. I never smell anything.

"I guess Sammy must have had an accident," Ms. Nancy said, shaking her head.

Ugh. Great. Guess that meant I was cleaning up the laundry room floor, and I didn't have a whole lot of time before I needed to get Caleb to school and myself to the newspaper. I mentally tried to outline all the steps I needed to get done before I rushed out the door.

Still. It didn't make sense. Sammy was housebroken. The only time he'd ever had an accident in the Horns' house was when Cliff and I were both out of town and they left Sammy at the house by himself and didn't put him in his crate. After they got home, they discovered he'd left a very nasty-looking "present" for them in the middle of the living room. And that was no accident. He was just mad.

Ms. Nancy told me not to worry with it, that she needed to scrub the laundry room floor anyway, and I could go on and drop Caleb off and head into work. I still was scratching my head over how Sammy could be the one responsible, but I couldn't think of any other explanation. Until I got a text from Cliff later that morning.

"You're never going to believe it."

"What?" I texted back.

"Mamaw peed in the laundry room."

"WHAT?"

When I got home that afternoon, the washer and dryer were in the garage. Ms. Nancy was in the laundry room on her hands and knees and everything smelled like bleach. *That* I could smell. She looked up at me and blew a strand of hair out of her face.

All I could do was offer a little grin.

"Seriously?"

"Yep!" Ms. Nancy said, going back to scrubbing. I noticed she was still in her pajamas.

Mamaw had shuffled out of her bedroom at nine o'clock as she always does, and when she noticed Ms. Nancy wiping down the floor, she confessed. Though it wasn't really a confession. It was more a statement of fact. I think when you're ninety-something, that's just the way it is.

"Weeelll," she had said, "I tried getting up last night to go to the bathroom, and I guess I got turned around and went the wrong way. Piddled all the way from the laundry room to the bathroom."

She announced it as though she'd just said she was having peanut butter and jelly for lunch. And then she headed to the kitchen to make her coffee. And I think that's when Ms. Nancy ordered Mr. Ray to move the washer and dryer out. The laundry room was getting a bath. In bleach.

And that's when I realized I hadn't stepped in water that morning. I'd stepped in…something else. Oh Lord.

I have learned a lot talking with Mamaw since she's been with us. She's told me a lot about her husband, Roy. He died many years ago, but not before they had celebrated over forty years of marriage. I'm not sure *celebrating* is the right word though, because as Mamaw tells it, their marriage and their life together were pretty hard.

Not long after they were married, Roy joined the army in preparation for the Korean War. But he never made it out of training before he suffered what the rest of the family refers to as "shell shock." I always assumed hearing this that he'd gone to war, but according to Mamaw, he never got there. He was in the hospital for months, and Mamaw moved to Atlanta from Mississippi to be near him. She rented a little room at a boarding-house across the street from the hospital and worked at a factory there in town to earn what little income she could.

He was never the same after he came home. Mamaw worked and earned the primary income because Roy couldn't keep a job for long before getting tired or bored of what he was doing and dreaming up something new to try. He had a bad temper and violent mood swings. At one point, he ran away with Mamaw's brother's wife. And yet she still took him back a few months later when he came crawling.

I'm not sure Mamaw saw her actions as submissive. But I do think she recognized commitment. And the ability to forgive, for she forgave both her husband and her sister-in-law. Maybe she thought of her daughter and son and decided they were better off with a flawed father than no father at all. Maybe deep down, she just loved him and wanted to help him however she could.

Her faith has to have played a part, as well. Though her worsening hearing and vision keep her from doing much anymore, occasionally she will go to church on Sunday mornings if Mr. Ray and Ms. Nancy are home. And she keeps her Bible by her bed for daily reading as well as a couple of devotional books Ms. Nancy changes out for her. Though she's never really said, I suspect her love for God played a big part in the love she kept for her husband.

Her story makes me think about a picture I saw of an elderly couple walking off toward the distance, hand in hand. The caption with the picture reads: "Want to know why we're still together? Because back in our day, when something was broken, you didn't throw it away. You fixed it."

Knowing the struggles Mamaw has faced in her life and in her marriage helps put my own marriage in perspective. Submission actually sounds a little easier now. I'm married to a great man, a husband who loves me, who wants the best for me as I want the best for him. How could I not be willing to help him?

For the last month, we've kept swimming. Cliff is enjoying his job, and I am still working at the paper and taking my classes online and saving as much as we can. But the job is about to go away.

As much as I feel like a quitter, I've recognized I'm in over my head when it comes to time and time management. What was supposed to be a part-time job feels more like three-fourths time, more than what I can put in, and for the money I'm making from it, I figured out I could write one freelance article a week and break even.

But this time, I asked Cliff.

And he didn't let me off the hook so easy.

"Look, you're the one who thought you could do the job and graduate school and everything else we have going on," he said as we discussed it in our room one night.

He was right. I knew the point he was making—I should have talked to him before I even asked for the first interview, and he probably would have helped me figure out then that I couldn't do it. If only I'd been willing to listen.

I thought about the verse in Ephesians that says, "Now as the church submits to Christ, so wives are to submit to their husbands in everything" (5:24).

That word *everything* feels mighty big. Maybe too big. But I think this verse means husbands are to show leadership and, as with any case of leadership, to have a leader, there must be a follower. Can I learn to follow my husband? The word *follow* doesn't feel so great either. What if he leads us somewhere where I don't think we should go? Or want to go?

But isn't that what trust is about? And if I trust that God has put my husband in my life, then shouldn't I trust my husband?

But then another thought hit me. Does my lack of trust at times actually keep my husband from embracing his God-given call as the leader of our household? Do I ever get in the way of him pursuing the role God intended for him? That's a question that's giving me pause. I'm so concerned with what following Cliff might do for me, that maybe I'm not thinking about what following Cliff might do for him.

Cliff told me he agreed I should quit the job. He was nice enough not to say "I told you so." Though I'm sure he was thinking it.

Telling Sheila was hard. I didn't like letting her down. She'd taken a chance on me, I knew, and she'd grown used to having me there in the short time I'd been there, which was less than a month. But it should have been a clue to both of us that this job wasn't meant to last long—I realized I'd never brought anything from home to put on my desk. In fact, I had told very few people I knew that I was working there.

I gave Sheila my two-week notice and I stuck to it. And as I walked out to the parking lot my last day of the job, I vowed to remember the lesson I'd learned. To value and respect my husband's input *before* I made another decision on my own.

Love *HIS* Way

I'm not so sure this whole submission experiment has gotten off to such a great start. I realize I'm trying harder at this moment to stay in the good graces of my mother-in-law than my husband, and something that should have been so basic as discussing a job with him before I actually applied for it, well, didn't happen.

I think I need a new game plan.

At least with the Proverbs 31 wife experiment I had a whole passage to refer to. Tasks to try, or at least goals to attempt. Submission feels much, much harder. And a little more confusing.

But I keep looking at this verse in Ephesians. I need some direction. I need an anchor, something to guide me. Something I can measure so I know if I'm hitting the target or I'm just way off. Because at the moment, I feel way off.

"Wives, submit to your own husbands as to the Lord."

It doesn't say submit to your husbands if you feel like it. Or when you want to. Or if you agree. It says submit to your husbands. The same way you submit to God.

The guys don't get off the hook. There are instructions in this passage for them as well, but at this moment, I have to figure out what my role is. Ultimately, I'm not responsible for my husband, I'm responsible for my actions, and if we're paying close attention to what the Bible says, Cliff is responsible for me and for our household. The more I think and pray about this, the more I find myself believing marital submission is not necessarily mutual submission. Mutual submission makes marriage sound like a contract or agreement. We are mutually exclusive. He stays exclusive to me; I stay exclusive to him. He treats me right; I'll treat him right. He gives me what I want; I'll consider giving him what he wants. Just kidding. Kinda.

What I can be sure of is that submission is not like the comic strip I saw the other day. A little boy and a little girl are playing outside, and the little girl says, "I know what we can play, let's play like we're getting married!"

The little boy scratches his head and asks, "Well, how do we do that?"

The little girl, with a great big smile on her face, says eagerly, "You promise to love, honor and cherish me…" and with another big smile she adds, "and I promise to let ya!"

Yeah, I'm pretty sure that's not how it's supposed to go. But maybe it does for a lot of us who are married.

How is it supposed to go, then?

I need a plan. I need some steps I can follow that will help keep me from wandering in a giant circle trying to nail down what submission looks like.

And I think Ephesians 5:22 offers a key.

How do we treat our husbands? How are we *supposed* to treat our husbands?

As we treat God. No, not treating our husbands *like* God. But with a similar attitude. Maybe similar actions. Husbands are told to love their wives just as Christ loved the church (Ephesians 5:25). We're told to submit to our husbands "as to the Lord."

God's called me to love my husband. And I realize that because I love God, I want to do what he's called me to do. I want to love my husband. I want to love God's way. Which means treating others, including my husband, the way God would, and maybe in a double meaning of sorts, also loving my husband in ways he responds to, not necessarily ways I would. To love His way. To love his way.

I pull out a notebook and jot down some words that form the acronym HIS.

Honor.

Intention.

Selflessness.

Words that describe what I want to do. How I should behave. Guides to keep me going forward.

When I love His way, God's way, it means I want to be honoring— both to God and to my husband. Stepping back and letting my husband take the lead, not because he's claimed it but because God's said it. Loving God enough to show honor and love to my husband. I think honor means showing respect to Cliff, even when I don't agree with something or when I want to rush ahead. Honoring Cliff means waiting and letting him lead.

Being intentional means I will consciously look at all the ways I can be submissive to my husband. How I can help without hindering, how I can assist without being so assertive I take over completely.

The act of being selfless may be the hardest one. But I think it goes back to seeing my role as a wife as a ministry, as a special calling that God has given me as I serve Cliff in his role as my husband. My theory and my hope is that as I work to serve more selflessly, I will see Cliff doing the same. And just as he sees me understanding and supporting his efforts, I'll see him leading me and our family in ways that make me feel cherished and not dominated.

That's my theory. But at this point, I have no idea if I'll be right.

Moving Parts

Our search for a house is in full swing, and it's both exciting and challenging at the same time. I typically have eyes for houses the way most kids have eyes for ice cream. Bigger and better is always on my wish list, but our bank account doesn't agree. So I'm trying hard to let Cliff take the lead on this one. The whole honor and respect thing. But it's not easy. A girl's got opinions, right?

A few days ago, he called driving home from work. When I glanced at my phone to answer it, I noticed the time. It was later than when he usually gets home.

"Hey," he said.

"Hey," I said, balancing my five-pound Old Testament textbook on my knees as I sat in my self-appointed study corner, our bed.

"So, you know that house we were looking at the other night online? The one that was way out in the country?"

I remembered. The house was empty and looked huge from the pictures we'd viewed online. Spacious, open layout with columns dividing specific areas of the house, such as the living room from the foyer. The kitchen was a good size. And while it would be at least a twenty to twenty-five minute trek into town for grocery shopping and other errands, the price was very low for the square footage.

"Well, I drove by there just now."

Everything else he said got lost. Cliff had gone and looked at a house without me. Our first house to look at, and he did it on his own. I wasn't happy. I took a deep breath.

"I thought we were going to look at that house together."

"I know, but I just thought I'd run over here and see since I was coming home from work. It's not the house for us," he said.

I could feel a little tension in my shoulders.

"OK, wait a second. First, you go out and look at the house without me, and now you're telling me it's no good, without letting me have a say in that decision?"

"It's right up on the main road," Cliff said. "Like, there's no yard, no space between the house and the highway. It's literally right there. I really was just trying to do a nice thing."

I tried to calm down. Why do I get so easily perturbed when it comes to things like that? It always feels like a struggle for territory or rights or wants, which is silly because Cliff is one of the sweetest men I've ever known. (OK, granted, we were both in our early twenties when we met and married so there weren't a whole lot of other instances to know other sweet guys. But I digress.)

I was disappointed the house was not the one for us, but more than that, I was a little disappointed in myself. This submission thing was not clicking as I hoped it would. Because as head of household, why shouldn't Cliff have the option of going to look at a house first before I came and looked at it with him? Does that sound as old-fashioned reading it as it did when I typed it just now? Because here's the question that I'm thinking about: Does submission to my husband as head of household apply to everything in our family and marriage—or is it just spiritual in nature? Is Cliff supposed to be the spiritual leader of our home and not necessarily the leader for everything else? Most of the women I know approach marriage with an egalitarian view—that the husband and wife are in the marriage fifty-fifty, equal partners, equal decision makers. This idea of complementarianism—a big word for traditional marriage where the husband is seen as head of household and the wife is seen as the helper—doesn't stack up well with current culture.

But I don't want to do what the culture says I should do. I want to do what God's Word says because that's my authority, that's my guide, that's my manual for navigating this crazy and wonderful thing we call life. And what I read when I look at the verses I've already mentioned is that it does seem the Bible supports specific roles in marriage. That husbands have specific things they focus on and wives have specific things we focus on.

Egalitarians might point to the verse in Ephesians where Paul writes we are to submit "to one another out of reverence for Christ" (5:21 NIV).

But when you look at the verse in context, it looks like Paul is talking about Christians within the church, not necessarily within a marriage. And I think there's a difference (though some folks don't want to see it as different, but that's a whole nother book).

Other verses describe what a husband is to do and how he is to behave and what a wife is to do and how she is to behave, and when I look at those side by side, I see a great set of instructions that seem to promote mutual love and respect—while still maintaining separate roles.

But I decided to do a little digging because, after all, I am trying to figure out how submission works in today's culture. And I ran across a study done earlier this year that offers an interesting perspective. A previous study, conducted in 2006, found that egalitarian marriages weren't necessarily so happy and that there was something to living in a more traditional, complementarian relationship. The more recent study was done in Norway, of all places, and found that happier relationships depended on the woman's happiness (I totally could have saved them the time and told them that)—and a woman wasn't always the happiest in a marriage that was fifty-fifty.

The Norwegian study showed that the divorce rate among couples who shared housework equally was 50 percent higher than those where women did most of the work. Their study showed that the more a man actually did in the home, the higher the divorce rate. But it contradicts another study in Great Britain that showed that couples who *did* split the chores and decided ahead of time who would be responsible for what, had more long-term success than others who went into their marriages without discussing those types of practical matters.

So, after looking at all of that, I'm still not sure whether it's necessary that Cliff have final say in such important decisions like buying a house. And I can't even begin to address the issue of him helping around the house. After all, right now we live with his mother.

But house hunting has begun. We've kept up a daily search on the Realtor app we both have on our phones, and there's one house in particular that Cliff has a definite opinion about. It looks like it's in foreclosure, as are several houses in the area, and while I'm a little leery about that, nothing seems to detract him from what he knows to be true.

The house has a shop.

Now, I've never understood why some men have this need to call a detached garage a shop. Maybe it's to communicate to women the importance of such a dwelling. We like *shopping*; well, they like to go to the *shop*. They use the shop to do manly things. Lift weights or work on cars or, in my husband's case, make things from wood. It's always been Cliff's dream to have a shop just like his dad had at one time. Cliff still remembers the days of being out in the garage (sorry, I'm calling it what it is) and hanging out with his dad building things.

So we find a Realtor and take our house hunting to the next level, from Internet searches to actual visits one Saturday afternoon while the Horns are out of town. The house with the shop is the first one we look at. It's pink. Looked a little different color on the website. Definitely outdated. But color can always be repainted, and I try to see past the fading pastel and look at the potential. The front door is the original, at least eight feet tall. It's old but classic. The house itself is a little bigger than our previous house in Nashville, especially when you add in the detached garage and the storage room. Four bedrooms, nice-size kitchen and dining area. There's a bedroom right off the kitchen that seems a little out of place since the rest of the rooms are all down a hall toward the back of the house. But it might make a great office for me or a game room for Caleb. The house is older, and the kitchen appliances are seriously dated. But right now, any space that we could call ours is looking pretty good.

We discover that the outdoor storage building, a standard feature for homes in this area, is a lot bigger than normal and was built by the original owners to house a one-chair beauty salon. So there's a sink, electricity, even a phone and cable line. It would need a lot of work, but it might even make a great office away from the house for me. Now I'm the one who starts dreaming.

Cliff's face lights up as we walk into the garage and a smile spreads across his lips. A long built-in wooden workbench lines one side, and white corkboard hangs on all four walls. Lots of space for him to use. Like the interior of the house, this space needs some TLC and a little work too.

While we do like the house, and we know the possibilities are good we can get it for lower than the asking price, we still follow our Realtor's suggestion and take a look at a few other houses. One in particular makes my heart skip a little beat. The walls are all a subtle beige and black wrought iron seems to be the central theme. Little black knobs in classic Louisiana fleur-de-lis design are on every top cabinet in the kitchen with solid black door pulls on the bottom ones. There's a custom black-and-white back-splash. The sinks have updated faucets. The yard out back is neat and pristine, with a little rock walkway leading from the backdoor toward a dark stately deck. It's beautiful. But very small. Five hundred square feet less than the older house Cliff likes. You know, the one with the shop.

We talk about it, weighing the pros and cons of each. The first house will require a lot of work, but it's bigger with more space to grow into. The second house is all ready to move into, but they're asking a whole lot more for it and it's a lot smaller—will we feel cramped a year from now?

As we discuss, I find myself subconsciously weighing how much I should insist and how much I should help. Am I *helping* my husband by offering my opinion? Can I offer an opinion without insisting? Can I help without trying to control the decision? Or have final say? From a practical standpoint, it seems to make more sense to go with the first house. I tell Cliff what I think, and he agrees without hesitation. Of course he would. It has a shop.

We discuss with Annie, our Realtor, what we'll offer, starting at $8,000 less than what the bank is asking for. While we're filling everything out, Annie calls the Realtor who is selling the property and finds out someone else is making an offer too. This is the part that makes me crazy. Running numbers and worrying whether we're making the right decision, whether we've offered enough to beat out the other party, whether we really have full confidence we can afford this house. Dealing with unemployment for three years might make anyone a little skittish, I think. But the paperwork is complete, and now we just wait and see.

Annie called us back the next day.

"Got bad news," she said. "I talked to the Realtor this morning, and the bank accepted the other offer. When the other buyer found out y'all were putting in an offer too, they upped theirs, and y'alls was lower than their original anyway."

Win some, lose some. I sighed and thanked her before hanging up, then called Cliff. I felt worse for him than for me. He had his heart set on that shop. He was disappointed, but we'd been disappointed before.

"If it's not meant to be our house, it's not meant to be," he said. "We'll keep looking."

I agreed with him, but I added one thing. "I think we need to take a step back," I said, surprising myself. "As much as I know we want our own place, I think we need to take our time. There's no sense in rushing things, no sense in getting into something we can't afford."

Ms. Nancy and Mr. Ray are still traveling, and we're not paying rent anymore since we're helping with Mamaw while they're gone. We can keep saving and keep looking for the house that we really want and not settle for something just because it's available.

Once again I felt like God was whispering a little lesson in all of this. Waiting on him, not rushing ahead, not trying to find the answer myself. Letting go. Maybe that is all part of what submission means too.

About a month has passed, and Cliff and I are trying to be patient as we work and save, and I do my best to try and be content in our circumstances.

I've been subbing more at the elementary school down the street. Mostly for the PE coaches. This is my first year to substitute teach, and I almost didn't go back after my second time. That day I'd filled in for a pregnant coach who needed to go to her doctor's appointment. She'd left very specific instructions with me to take the kids out to run and to be very conservative with their bathroom breaks. Most of them, she wrote in her notes, should have already had time to go before PE class, and they will try to get out of running by going to the bathroom.

Sure enough, the kids would run one or two laps and come to me asking for a bathroom break. I tried to be judicial. The challenge for me as the substitute was to keep an eye on the kids running around this big fenced-in sidewalk that circled a man-made lake. The door to the school was locked, which meant kids needed keys to get in, and the door was about fifty feet from where I needed to stand to watch the runners.

So I devised a system. The kids who absolutely needed to go to the bathroom could stand in line at the door, and as one kid came back out, the next kid could go in. I could keep my eye on the kids running (we'd already had two boys fall because they were horse playing) and we'd get through these classes, no problem.

I thought it was a brilliant plan and a successful day of subbing until I got a call from the school principal the next day. A little girl had wet herself. Seriously. I'd made a child pee on herself because she'd waited too long to go to the bathroom.

Now, the girl had never said anything to me, and I had no idea who she even was, but the parents had definitely said something. Understandably. The principal was very gracious and said it wasn't a problem, he just needed to let me know. And I learned new words that day to ask students: "Is it an emergency?" I vowed that from then on, no matter what the teacher notes said, no kid was going to be denied going to the bathroom. I was just the substitute. They didn't pay me enough to make a child wet her pants.

But still, I felt terrible. And to help me feel better, that Friday night Cliff took me on a Home Depot date while Caleb stayed with Nana and Papaw for a movie.

Home Depot dates are our cheap dates. They usually consist of dinner at a local hamburger joint that has really good burgers and nachos with a side of jalapeños. Comfort food that will help me forget about the Substitute Nazi I had unknowingly been this week. Cliff couldn't help but laugh at me, but he was partly to blame too. He'd substituted a little before he'd been hired full-time at his new job, and he was always coming home telling me how he'd told kid after kid no when it came to extra bathroom breaks. Leave it to my luck, though, to get the kid with the tiny bladder. After we finished eating, we got back in the car and drove over to Home Depot for our biweekly dreaming of house things and what we would do one day when we actually had a house again. On the way, I took a look, as I did so often these days, at the Realtor app.

That was odd.

"Hey, hon, the house is on here!"

The pink house, the house with Cliff's shop, the one we'd lost out on, was listed.

"Did they not take it off?" Cliff asked.

We decided to check with our Realtor and find out. I sent her a quick text with the address and asked her if she could find out what the status was. Three minutes later, my phone rang.

"You're not going to believe this," Annie said.

The house was back on the market. After the other buyers' offer was accepted, Annie said the listing agent told her the buyers flaked out and never submitted the rest of the paperwork. So less than twenty-four hours earlier, the bank put the house back on the market.

Cliff and I couldn't believe what had happened. Could this maybe be a sign this was supposed to be our house, just in God's timing and not ours? We told Annie we'd talk it over and give her a call back. We definitely wanted to make an offer; we just weren't sure what we wanted that number to be.

We discussed it while we walked around Home Depot, and we decided by the time we got home to talk to Ms. Nancy.

Ms. Nancy is like Midas in a blond wig. The woman knows money and how to make it work. I'd hoped by living with her that some of that knowledge would rub off a little, but no such luck. But now I just hoped we could get her help and advice. The first time, we tried to do it on our own; this time, we were going to tap every resource we could.

Ms. Nancy was sitting in the living room when we got home. After explaining to her what had just happened, we showed her the house online, and her face got that look it always does when she's thinking over numbers in her head. After about thirty minutes of researching online to find past appraisals and values, and after scratching out what our income was and what would be a comfortable monthly mortgage payment, Ms. Nancy announced what she would offer for the house if she were wanting to buy it. Her number was over $15,000 less than what the current asking price was, and a few thousand less than what we'd offered before.

Cliff and I looked at each other. It sounded nice, but surely there was no way the bank would go for it.

Ms. Nancy chuckled and smiled her big smile. "If they want to get a house off their hands, they will. Banks are not in the real estate business."

Our Realtor was not as thrilled when we told her what we'd decided to offer.

"That's really low," Annie said. "I'm not sure they're going to go for that—that's lower than what you offered before. Don't you think you want to go a little higher?"

"No, that's the number we want to offer," I said. "They can always come back and counter, or they can say no, and we'll keep looking."

"Well, I don't think they'll go for it, but if that's what you want me to offer them, then OK."

Before she got off the phone, she explained that since it was a bank situation, it would probably be at least three or four days before we heard anything. They weren't going to think it necessary to respond to us within twenty-four hours.

We told her we understood.

Five days later we finally got an answer. All that waiting, all that wondering, and it came down to one phone call. Annie's voice could barely hide her disappointment.

"Hi, Sara. I just heard from the listing agent. You got the house. We need to go ahead and move on this paperwork and get this done…"

As she went over what we needed to do next, I could feel my heart beating faster. We got the house. We got the house! We were going to be homeowners again!

I tried ignoring the fact Annie hadn't said congratulations, hadn't acted happy for us, and had got off the phone as quickly as possible. Nothing was going to steal our joy that we now had a place we would call our own—and at a great price we could afford.

And we owed it all to Ms. Nancy. I quickly called Cliff.

"I think I know what I want for my birthday," I blurted out.

"Huh? What?" My birthday was in March, about thirty days away.

"*A house!* We got the house!"

A little later, I walked into the Horns' house and called out, looking for Ms. Nancy.

She was in the living room, in her usual spot at three o'clock, waiting for Mr. Ray to wake up from his nap so he could bring her coffee. She gazed up at me sleepily.

"Stand up," I said, with a big smile on my face.

"Why?" she said, nervously getting to her feet.

I wrapped my arms around her. "Because we got the house!"

It was time to start packing.

More Changes

Four years ago, my mom moved to where we lived in Nashville, just a couple of months before Cliff left for his first deployment. The timing seemed right. She and my dad had divorced two years before, and with my brother, the youngest of our family, at that time a West Point cadet and no other family around, she'd tired of being by herself. It was hard to go to church as the single divorced person when seemingly all of her friends came with their husbands. She was ready for a change. With Cliff deploying, she saw the move as a good kill-two-birds-with-one-stone incentive—she could be near family, and I could get her help and support while Cliff was gone.

After not living around any family for most of our marriage, it was an adjustment for me having her so close by. But she loved spending time with Caleb, her only grandson. The apartment she rented for most of that time was just four minutes or so from our neighborhood, and when she decided to buy a townhouse, that too was just down the road. But then just two years later, we moved away to Louisiana, and once again she was alone.

Until I got her text.

"I've been let go," it said, and my heart sank. Her job at a medical insurance corporation had not always been the easiest, but she'd worked hard in her position. Plus, I knew she couldn't afford not to have a job. The worst part, though, was that she owned a townhouse with a mortgage. She was stuck, or at least it seemed that way.

We talked by phone later that night. If you'd asked me when I was a kid who was the strongest woman I knew, my mom would come instantly to mind. She was the kind you said came from "good stock" because she'd overcome a lot in her lifetime. The marriage she'd lived through had not been the kindest or easiest. She'd come from a family where love was often replaced with anger and threats and violent outbursts, and when she met my dad, she was hungry for it. My dad, unfortunately, came from a family where love just wasn't shown openly, and so he didn't really know how to offer what Mom needed.

I watched their twenty-nine years of inability to understand or communicate end like a painfully smoldering brush fire that scorched and destroyed and eventually just put itself out, never quite able to ignite with the love both of them needed. But Mom stayed strong for the kids, and I remember watching her do what needed to be done, making sure we got what we needed, even when she was painfully aware of what she herself didn't have. But she was strong.

After the divorce, though, she lost some of that strength, and I'd slowly, resignedly accepted it over time. I understood she needed help, someone else to lean on. Most of us do at some point in our lives. And in Mom's case, that person was usually me, though during my workaholic phases, I don't know if I was always there. Most of the time, I'm pretty sure I wasn't.

I wanted to be now, though, and as we talked, I knew she needed to be closer to family. We weighed the possibility of her moving back to our little town. It seemed an impossible jump to take, considering she had a mortgage to pay, and with a struggling economy, we had no assurance her townhouse would sell any time soon.

She had a little time and unemployment benefits that would help a little, and I told her to give herself a few days to get over what had happened, push aside the panic she was feeling, and then dream a little about what the possibilities could be. Another job there? A job here? Something would work out.

Three days later I called her. Clay, my brother-in-law, was moving from the upstairs apartment he currently lived in to the downstairs apartment below him. The apartment he was leaving was small but comfortable, and it was in a relatively safe area of town and near the police station. She could drive down and check it out and maybe explore some job options too. I also offered to take a look at her résumé and told her I'd start scouring job sites for her.

I started putting her résumés out there, and she started sorting her stuff. If she did move, she would probably need to get rid of some things.

That weekend, Mom came down and stayed with us at the Horns. It worked out since my in-laws were traveling. Mom could stay in their room and come and go as needed. The first order of business was to check out the apartment.

The little group of rentals was owned by a couple of men who went to our church and had been business partners for a long time. Mom had been in a Sunday school class years before with at least one of them and his wife, and it didn't take long for them to agree to hold it for her should she decide she wanted to move down.

We met Mr. Johnny at the apartment and followed him up the stairs. He assured us it would be freshly painted before she moved in, and there was some good-natured teasing as he and Mom got caught up while she looked around. There was a kitchen, a little dining area, a living room, and a bedroom and master bathroom off the living room. It was small but cozy. But there was a problem. At least I thought there was a problem.

As we checked out the kitchen, opening up cabinets and talking about the amount of storage, I realized it was missing something vitally important.

"Mom, it doesn't have a dishwasher!" I said. "Is that going to be a deal breaker?"

Mom chuckled and gave me a knowing look. I still remembered the times I'd whined and carried on when she'd made me do the dishes as a kid—and the few times I'd had to use our sink instead of the dishwasher.

"Sara, I've had these hands long before you were born," she said. "I know how to wash dishes."

Look, every gal's got her priorities. I'd done my time without a dishwasher when Cliff and I lived in married housing during college. That was a time I did not want repeated.

By the time Mom left later that week, she'd already put a deposit down for the apartment and interviewed for an admin position at the local hospital's nursing home. Things were looking up for her, and though I was nervous at the changes coming, I was excited for her too.

Three weeks later, she pulled her U-Haul into town.

She still had no job and no renter for her home back in Nashville, but she was here. And as I welcomed her with a big hug, I had no idea her arrival would lead to the biggest fight Cliff and I had ever had.

The Really-Not-So-Submissive Fight

Mom arrived on a Friday, and that night I took her to a concert where a Christian comedian and a singer were both headlining. I'd asked Cliff if he was OK with it, and he was, once I'd explained that Mom could really use some fun (and frankly, so could I). So we went and had a great time.

The next day was moving day. Of course, Cliff had to drive to his drill weekend in New Orleans. Because of the navy, that man has been saved from moving boxes more times than I can count. But he asked his dad and brother to help, and a few of our guys from Sunday school were nice enough to lend a hand too.

We got a late start due to rain. I called off the moving help until the downpour stopped, and instead, I brought in what boxes I could from the truck. I figured even if we had to wait on the furniture, at least we could get some of the boxes up.

But there was a problem besides the rain. Mom had a whole lot of stuff. And Mom's new place was small. A storage facility wasn't an option. And our house wasn't going to be ours for another several weeks.

Looking at Mom's new apartment, I couldn't help but feel a little sad for her. Everything was a lot smaller than what she'd had in Tennessee. The space was already filling up with boxes, and the furniture wasn't even in yet. Before the move, I'd tried encouraging her to get rid as much as she could. But I could already tell she hadn't gotten rid of enough.

I remembered the house she used to have. It sits just behind the high school, and it's where I spent the last two years before Cliff and I married, at least when I was home from college. I remembered her bell collection and other trinkets she collected, all kept in a beautiful display case.

Those had been long discarded. I recalled the big kitchen she enjoyed. The kitchen in this apartment was a whole lot smaller.

But Mom was determined to start this new adventure with hope, and though she recognized the space was small, she was happy to call it hers. Even if she did miss her Tennessee closets.

The weather finally started cooperating, and brother-in-law Clay made his way out of his apartment to come help about the same time his dad and the other guys started arriving. The work started briskly, and what little furniture Mom brought with her made its way up the stairs and into the space.

Until it came time for the piano.

The piano was a sore subject. Mom and I had already talked about it. She'd had it ever since I could remember—I'd practiced my piano lessons on it when I was seven, I knew that much. When I got older, Mom would play hymns or praise and worship songs or Christmas songs, and I'd sing along, usually one of us singing harmony to the other. I knew Mom had a lot of special memories built up in that piano. But there was a problem. Actually two problems.

It was too heavy, and there was no way that piano was going to make the corner of the second-floor landing to get in the door.

The guys were resistant to even try, and Mom was frustrated that they wouldn't.

Finally, when almost everything else was in the house and there was barely any room to walk, let alone move in a three-hundred-pound piano, Mom relented. She agreed to let us take the piano over to the Horns' place until we moved into our house, and then the piano would come with us. I talked to Cliff by phone, and he told me he'd get a couple of guys to help after he got back from drill the next day. Mom wasn't too happy about leaving the piano out in the truck, even for twenty-four hours, but there was no other option.

After church the next morning, I headed over to Mom's to help unpack. She'd already gotten a lot of the kitchen done, but her entire bedroom was filled with boxes, and there was barely any room to move things out into the living room. She'd sold her bed before she moved, which was smart since she would have had no place to put it, but I felt bad she was sleeping on her couch.

Things got interesting, though, the more I started getting into boxes.

"Mom, what's this?" I asked, holding up a plain, bright-green wicker basket. I knew what the basket was. I knew where it came from. I just couldn't believe my mother still had it.

"Oh, that's one of the baskets we used in your wedding," she said.

"Mom, that was fourteen years ago. Why do you still have this?"

"'Cause it's special!"

OK. I continued going through boxes. Lots of little stuff, everywhere. Knickknacks and pillows, an entire Barbie doll collection of my sister's, and…a fishing pole? I pulled out the small fishing pole wrapped up in a blanket.

"Mom?" I held up the pole, a big question mark on my face.

"Oh, that was the fishing pole your brother had when he was twelve," Mom said.

"Seriously? Then why do you still have this?" My brother hadn't lived at home since he'd left at eighteen for West Point almost seven years ago.

"Well, Sara, he may want it someday." I could hear in her voice that she was getting irritated with me.

I thought about my brother, the army captain, who spent time outdoors only when he had to.

"Mom, I'm pretty sure Jonathan doesn't need this. Let's get rid of it."

"No, we need to at least ask him if he wants it."

Oh Lord. I felt as though I was watching the beginning of an episode of *Hoarders*.

I texted my brother. *Mom still has your fishing pole from when you were 12. Remember it? Do you still want it?*

Oh yeah? he texted back. *What does it look like?*

Oh brother.

It's a fishing pole. For kids.

Oh, OK…lol. Give it to Caleb.

Great. More stuff for us to bring with us to our house.

I was able to convince Mom to put more in the trash pile or giveaway pile. Including the green wicker basket she'd kept for fourteen years. We were slowly making progress.

But we still had the piano in the truck. And Mom, already not happy about how many of her things she was once again having to let go of, was getting more and more irritated about the piano. And I was getting more and more stressed about the whole thing.

I called Cliff, who was finally on his way home from his drill.

"Are you almost here? We need to get the piano moved over to your parents' house."

"Yeah, I'm almost into town now."

Right or wrong, I felt extremely responsible for ensuring that my mom's move was a good one, and this piano had turned into one big major issue. The sooner we got it over to the Horns', the better. But Cliff seemed to be taking his time.

"I'm gonna meet a couple of the guys over at CrossFit, and after the workout, we'll come get it."

"Cliff, we need to get the piano moved."

"Sara, I know we do. We'll do it after the workout."

'Cause that makes sense. Let's go wear ourselves out with an extreme fitness workout and then move a piano.

Rational or not, I could feel myself getting mad. Extremely mad. Maybe because I'd spent all weekend unpacking boxes and walking up and down stairs, and the one major thing I really needed my husband for, he wasn't there right away to help me. Or he at least didn't seem that concerned. Or didn't share my concern.

I needed him to be there for me. Not after CrossFit, not after his other plans, but *right now*.

And he wasn't.

An hour went by, and Mom and I started to wrap up for the night. We were both tired, but we'd made a lot of progress. I felt like I'd avoided a hoarders' intervention with her, though barely. I hauled a bunch of the trash downstairs and out to the road to be picked up by the trash crew the next day. And then I tried calling Cliff.

No answer.

I sat upstairs with my mom for another half hour and tried calling again. Still no answer. This was ridiculous.

"Sara, he'll get here soon, I'm sure," Mom said, her eyes showing concern. She could see my eyes were glaring.

"He should have already been here," I snapped.

Have you ever witnessed an accident and everything suddenly started moving in slow motion? Like it's all underwater and you can see what's about to happen and there's nothing you can do about it?

Yeah, that was me at just that moment. I was in anger overload and about to boil over.

I got in my car and drove over to the Horns'. I tried calling Cliff again. Still no answer.

I walked into the house. Caleb was watching television. He'd already eaten something Ms. Nancy had fed him. Mr. Ray was out by the pond feeding fish.

I didn't know what made me more angry—that Cliff was late getting the one thing done I'd asked him to do or that I couldn't even get him on the phone.

I wanted to fuss. I wanted to fume. I wanted to pitch a big ole hissy fit. But there was no place to go where I could just be mad without someone asking me what was wrong. So I left. I got back in my car and drove back onto the road. And as I pulled up to the stoplight of the main intersection just outside my in-laws' subdivision, there was the U-Haul. With Cliff behind the wheel and two other guys sitting next to him in the cab.

And that's when my phone rang. It was Cliff. And like a brat, I refused to answer it.

I knew I wasn't being submissive. I knew I was being just plain ridiculous. But what happened to him helping me? What happened to him putting me first at a time I really needed him to?

It was dinnertime and I was hungry and I went to the only place I knew I could get a little peace and lick my wounds. The local sushi place. I don't even like the sushi there. But it was quiet and it was dark and as I sat there by myself, brooding while I waited for my food to arrive, I tried to think about this whole submission thing.

Obviously, I wasn't being very submissive. But I'm not sure Cliff was being very head of household. Because for as many verses as there are in the Bible about wives respecting and showing honor and support to their husbands, there are also many verses that instruct a husband to show love (Ephesians 5:25) and to do everything he can to care for and honor his wife (1 Peter 3:7).

I think more than anything, my feelings were hurt. I'd worked so hard lately to put Cliff first, to be kind, to look out for his interests, his needs, his wants. And the one moment I'd really needed him to step up for me and be there…he just wasn't. Not in the way I'd needed him to be. Yes, he got the job done, but on his timetable, and not mine.

And maybe that was the biggest issue. Maybe that was what had me so frustrated.

He hadn't jumped when I said jump. He hadn't moved when I'd demanded he move.

And maybe that was totally missing the point of submission and whole head of the household concept. I should have been more patient. I should have been more loving. Maybe more understanding. I was forgetting my game plan—to honor him, to be intentional, to be selfless.

Yeah, I definitely wasn't being selfless at the moment.

But I'm not a robot, am I?

Still. I knew I couldn't control his actions, but I could control mine.

My phone rang again and it was Cliff. I picked it up.

"Hey, where have you been?"

"Where have you been?" I asked, and not very nicely, I should add.

"Well, I got the piano picked up at your mom's, and we took it over to my mom's and now we're driving the truck back over."

"OK. Thanks." I was still angry.

"So where are you?" I could hear the irritation in his voice.

"I'm eating sushi," I snapped back, feeling slightly silly in my "so there" tone.

"OK…"

"I'll be home in a few minutes."

When I walked into the house twenty minutes later, I immediately made a beeline into our room. That's one drawback about living with a whole bunch of other people—you have no privacy to just have a really good fight. Cliff and I sat on the bed. I tried to explain how I'd felt. He tried to explain how he felt. Neither one of us felt we were completely in the wrong. Which kind of irritated me. But I knew, ultimately, I needed to step back on this one. Even if I was still a little angry.

We went to bed that night still not completely talking, the situation still not completely resolved.

Cliff got up early and left for work without us saying much to each other. I didn't like the feeling. And I knew I wasn't hitting my target of loving God's way. I wasn't even on the board. Caleb was at school, and the

Horns had left to take Mamaw to Texas for a few days to see her sister. I needed to do the right thing.

I sent Cliff a text and told him I was sorry about what had happened. That's something I realize I need to do more of. Say I'm sorry. Often, Cliff is the one who comes to me first. And he's noticed. So I asked him if we could have lunch. He texted back that he'd like that, and I drove into Baton Rouge and met him for lunch. For sushi.

He sat across the table from me, and as the waiter walked away with our order, I said, "I'm sorry. I was upset, and I got angry and I blew up."

"I'm sorry too," he said.

We talked about my feeling that he hadn't been there when I needed him most and his feeling that he had but I'd seriously overreacted (which, let's be honest, he was probably more right than I was).

After our discussion had quieted, and the sushi rolls were all eaten, I felt a little better.

Cliff sat back in his seat. "So when are we starting this submission thing?" he asked, a slight grin across his face.

Ouch. I totally got his point. But it still stung a little bit.

I want to serve God in the roles he's placed me in as a wife and mom. I do believe there's an order to marriage, to life, to the plan God has for me. I want to be a great wife to Cliff and a great mom to Caleb. I want to be a helper to Cliff too. This whole submission idea still feels like there's a lot of tension in it—there's a pushing and pulling to be right—or to give up my rights. But I don't think that's what God intends.

It's hard sometimes to listen to Cliff, especially when I think I'm right and he's not. Does God really expect me to just keep my mouth shut? What's the point of being a helper to my husband if I do that, even when I think there may be a better way or a better answer? And as a leader, shouldn't my husband be willing to hear other opinions? Isn't that the mark of someone who leads well?

I know I have a lot to learn.

A Chain of Command

If there is a blessing in this whole experimental process, it's that Cliff and I are talking a lot more about what it means to be married and what our roles as a married couple should look like (or how we want them to look). We're looking more closely at what we're each doing and how we do it, and how we help our spouse.

This is big. In almost the decade and a half we've been married, this hasn't happened before.

Before, the closest we ever came to discussing roles was who was responsible for taking out the trash and doing the dishes. And even then, that was sometimes up for debate. Especially when one of us just didn't feel like it. Sure, each of us helps. But someone needs to lead. And when it comes to housework and the household, that's usually fallen on me, even when I was just as busy or busier than Cliff. He helps when he feels like it, but if it's going to get done, it usually falls to me to do it, even when I *don't* feel like it.

The Proverbs 31 experiment helped me with my attitude on this. Before, I became extremely resentful when the laundry piled up and there was no attempt on Cliff's part to help with it. I'd get angry. Was he blind? Did he really not see that we were going to be naked by the end of the week if someone didn't throw the clothes into the washer and hit "start"? Did he really not mind using towels until they were crunchy? Who went and said I was laundry queen without my consent? Because I didn't like doing the laundry any more than he did.

But something happened as a result of the last experiment. I started changing my attitude. I stopped seeing laundry as some offense to my rights as a woman or a wrong I needed to right, and I just started seeing it as a small blessing I could do for my family. I changed my attitude and I stopped complaining or insisting that Cliff do the laundry at least once a week. I just did the laundry. And when I needed help, I asked for it. I didn't get upset. I didn't pitch a fit as I passed by the laundry and saw yet again that "someone" hadn't done it (that nonexistent maid I like to get mad at some days just so I can blame someone else: "We really need to fire her!"). I just did it. I chose to be that someone. I realized someone needed to do it, and what was my excuse? Was refusing on principle really helping anyone?

As my attitude and actions changed, what I saw over time was that Cliff's attitude and actions changed too. And we worked together more as a team. But ultimately, I take responsibility for the laundry. I *am* the Laundry Queen. And proud of it (on most days). I make sure my family doesn't roam the streets without clothes. It's a gift.

I've grown to understand there is a need for order when it comes to certain things. Maybe many things. I'm just not sure what it looks like. Who establishes it? What does "head of household" mean anyway?

Cliff and I've discussed it. As we get ready to move into our own house, just days away now, Cliff has a theory.

"I think the whole head of household thing is like the chain of command we have in the military," he said as we cleaned up dishes one night. Cliff's parents were out of town and Mamaw had shuffled back to her room to call her sister in Texas. "The commanding officer is in charge. He doesn't necessarily do all the work himself, but he is ultimately responsible. He also doesn't spend all his time barking orders and telling everyone else what to do. A good CO has to lead by example. I think that's what a head of household has to do too."

"So I'm like the first mate or something?" I asked. "You're the captain?"

"Yeah," Cliff said, smiling. "And when the captain isn't around, the first mate keeps the ship going, and when the captain is around, they work together toward the goals and objectives the captain sets."

It was an interesting analogy. Helpful in a lot of ways. Except I didn't always clearly see any goals or objectives set by my sweet laid-back husband. I used to drive him crazy around the first of every year when I asked him to talk about what we'd achieved the year before and what goal he wanted to set for the next year. He hated stuff like that, and I'd stopped trying to pull it out of him about the fifth year of our marriage. Usually I was the one saying we needed to do something or we needed to plan for something. So how did that whole captain leading thing work again?

Still, at least he was thinking about it. And maybe as his first mate, it was part of my job as a helper to help him think about those things he might not always focus on. I did feel a little lighter in my heart and my spirit when I thought about it like that. Leading our family wasn't my job. It was Cliff's. It was my job to help him. And maybe it was his job to let me.

I walked out to the garage to grab another box to pack. I'd already packed up Caleb's room, and we were working on ours. Most of our stuff was still in storage, but there were boxes stacked up in the living room and our room. It wouldn't be long now and we would be in our own place again. And maybe that's where the real test would be.

What Does Helping Look Like Anyway?

We moved into the house right before spring break. I was glad Cliff took a few days off to help get everything settled. My mom helped with a little of the unpacking, and a few of our friends and a few of Cliff's friends from CrossFit helped move furniture.

I'm excited for Mom. She got some great news this week. Just as she was starting to panic about her situation—no job, a mortgage to pay in Tennessee—God did a miracle. On the same day, she got a call for a job interview (and she starts the job at the end of the month) and notice that someone was going to lease her townhome. An amazing answer to prayer and one—make that two—less worries off my mind for my mom.

The house we bought is about twenty years old, and since it was a foreclosure, it has a lot of things we need to touch up and work on. But it's ours. The neighborhood is quiet and established. We have a big backyard, and Cliff has his shop, though not a whole lot to fill it with at the moment. The kitchen is big, with large oversize windows that run from ceiling to floor, letting in lots of sunshine. I'm not crazy about the stovetop and tiny oven that look like they are the original ones that came with the house, but those can be updated over time. The floors are wood laminate (the cheap kind, not the real) except where it's carpeted in the bedrooms. There are big built-in bookshelves in the living room with a mantel over a fireplace. The windows go from floor to ceiling in here as well and look across to the long narrow foyer that leads to the front door.

This first month I worked hard to unpack everything quickly and make our new house a home. I'm not one to live in boxes and I had fun getting to decide where things went. My choice. My decision. Now that the boxes have been put out to the curb, our storage unit has been closed out, and Cliff and Caleb are back at work and school, I'm working on establishing the routines I've always wanted to have.

And not doing very well.

Because while we were moving everything in and getting settled, life still went on. Bills still have to be paid and taxes have to get done. I'm working on another writing project. Finishing grad classes for this semester. Getting ready for new speaking events.

Frustration is starting to set in because I'm really trying to be tuned in to being Cliff's helper, since I see that as the primary definition for a wife. But it feels like Cliff still helps me more than I help him.

For instance, I got upset this morning because Cliff asked me what we were having for dinner. That was item 52 on the list I have running in my head, and I was only on item 1. When he does this, it throws me off, and my first instinct is to stress out. Today was no exception.

So he offered to cook. Which just made me crankier because aren't I the one who should cook?

"I want to help you," he told me.

I stopped in the middle of our kitchen and gave him a look. "But I'm supposed to help you. And I don't feel like I'm doing that very well."

He sighed and leaned against the kitchen counter with his hands in the tops of his pockets and looked at me.

"Come here," he said.

I looked at him doubtfully, but stepped forward anyway, and he put his arms around me and pulled me close.

"You do help me, Sara," he said, smiling. "You did the laundry yesterday so I have clothes to wear today. You did our *taxes* and got us a great refund. You made dinner last night when neither one of us really felt like cooking and could just have easily spent thirty dollars on takeout. You do help." He pulled back and looked at me. "And as head of household, I help too. It's not my job to sit around and do nothing. It's my job to make sure the household is good. And if I can help by making dinner, that's what I'm going to do."

We decided on hamburgers and homemade french fries using the potatoes we have. And once again, I sighed a prayer of thanks for my husband.

I do wonder though if I have once again taken on too many things. Helping to coach kindergarten cheerleaders has just finished, and now

Cliff and I are thinking about getting involved on Sunday mornings with the children's service. I'm still speaking, still writing. I'm almost done with the graduate classes I signed up for this semester, though truth be told it's been even harder than I thought it would be, and I haven't put near enough time into studying or writing my end of class papers as I should have. I'm managing to keep the house clean and looking nice, and yes, laundry is done *every day*. I can thank my mother-in-law for that little habit.

But I have to wonder—can the good or great principle apply to our homes and our families? All of these things are good, but are they the best and greatest choices for our family? For my husband? For me?

Cliff and I slipped into bed one night late, and as we lay there, I said, "I see this whole idea of submission as being a helper, but I don't necessarily know if there's any way I could be doing it differently than what I'm already doing." I asked him what he thought.

Cliff thought for a moment, and I laid my head on his chest and listened to him breathe. "I think it's like Maslow's Hierarchy of Needs."

Huh? My husband always surprises me.

"Everyone has basic needs that need to be met, and you do that for us. I think you're looking at this too hard."

"Yeah, but I'm supposed to be helping. What about with your job?"

Cliff chuckled. "I don't think you can come to work with me and do estimates, Sara."

He may have a point. But as I rolled over to go to sleep, I couldn't help but think I could be doing more. I started making a list in my head.

1. Pray for him. Every single day. If that's the only thing I do, I need to do it. I know that prayer works and that it's important.

2. Manage our finances better. Develop a clear budget and keep him in the loop and talking about it regularly.

3. Stay organized. When I'm not organized, when everything's cluttered and out of sorts, I get out of sorts. Being out of sorts does not help my husband. Which reminds me to go back to number 1.

4. Be more intentional about bringing in income. We need

extra income. But I'm not sure how helpful this is. Is this more for Cliff or for me?

5. Keep the house and laundry going. I definitely do a lot better in this area than I used to. But trying to do it in tandem with number 4 becomes challenging.

6. Help him stay on task with lists and projects. It's a nice thought, right? That's helping, isn't it?

7. Help him grow spiritually. Not so sure about this one. I still can't be the Holy Spirit to him. Maybe I should just go back to number 1.

Who Does What?

I had a chance to run to Baton Rouge for a few errands today so I stopped off at the Christian bookstore and looked around for a little bit. I found a great devotional written for Caleb's age that I thought we might be able to do as a family. I stood there in the aisle for a long time though. Was I being pushy by buying this? Or was I being a helper? Or was I stepping into head-of-household territory? Because, let's just be honest, was Cliff ever going to get around to looking for a family devotional? I didn't think he would. I was pretty sure he wouldn't. I had a plan. I could just bring it home and leave it in some inconspicuous place and make him think it was his idea.

"Hey babe," he would say, picking up the devotional he'd found, I don't know, sitting on top of the toilet. "Why don't we do this super great devotional together?"

"Well, husband of mine and head of our household," I would say, "that's a wonderful idea!"

And God would smile down on all of us, and we'd have our wonderful little family devotional moment like you might see in a Norman Rockwell painting.

I bought the book. But it didn't exactly go as I'd planned.

He called from work just as I was walking in the door and asked me how my day went, and I just blurted out, really fast, "I found a really cool family devotional I thought we might be able to do with Caleb."

There was silence.

"Uh, why didn't you ask me about it first?" Cliff asked.

"What do you mean, why didn't I ask you first?"

"I mean, why didn't you call me from the store before you bought it? Maybe I might have wanted to have some input on what we got. Did you ever think about that?"

Seriously? We were going to fight over a devotional?

"Well, I didn't call you because, um, I didn't think you'd want to do it."

Did I have to ask him about everything?

"OK, so why didn't you call me and ask?"

Blinking lights were going off in my brain. *Head of household…head of household…*

"Because I wanted us to do it and I didn't think you would."

"But don't you think it would have been a good idea to call?"

"Not if you were going to say no!"

By then both of us were chuckling at the ridiculousness of the entire thing. I placed the book on the corner of the desk in the kitchen. And there it sat. We still haven't started family devotions. I guess I learned my lesson. When Cliff wants to do them, we'll do them. I think back to my list I made earlier. I can't be his Holy Spirit. I can't be his Holy Spirit.

My brother just got married at West Point Military Academy. It was a beautiful ceremony. Caleb and I flew out for it, along with my mom and the rest of the family. Cliff, unfortunately, couldn't go because he had a mandatory drill weekend.

Caleb was asked to be a junior groomsman, and he looked so handsome and grownup in his tux. I was sad Cliff couldn't come and very glad to get home and see him Sunday night. I knew that the skipper had come for a visit, and I suspected there was some news coming that I wasn't going to like. The fact Cliff hadn't said anything when I'd asked him how the weekend had gone just heightened my suspicions, and so Monday night, as we stood in the kitchen getting dinner ready, I turned and looked at him.

"So, are you going to tell me how your drill weekend went?"

Cliff looked at me and smiled. But I knew that smile and I knew that look. It didn't mean happy news. I took a big breath and stood back against the stove with my arms folded.

"Tell me."

Cliff took a step forward and spoke softly so Caleb wouldn't hear from the next room. "I thought about telling you yesterday, but I didn't want to, not with how excited you were talking about the wedding and all." He paused before he spoke again. "We're on the list."

I nodded and sighed again. "When?"

"Next June. It's battalion-wide. To Afghanistan. It's a count-the-nails kind of mission. We're just going to help wrap everything up."

Just under a year away. Cliff had missed Caleb's tenth birthday. Now it looked like he would miss his thirteenth. And another Thanksgiving. Another Christmas.

Nothing made it easier to hear about another deployment. It didn't matter how many times we'd gone through this already, it never got easier. In some ways I think it gets a little harder because we know what's coming. The good-byes. The longing. The disappointment in what he misses while he's away. As a mom, my biggest worry is always Caleb. Each time he was a little older and each time it had gotten just a little harder. He was going to be at the age where he really needed his dad. I could feel the tears already forming, and for a few seconds, I gave in.

Cliff pulled me close and held me.

"I know," he murmured, his lips against my forehead.

I looked up at him and tried to put on my brave-soldier face. "OK, well, we have time, and besides, anything can change between now and then. We'll just take it as it comes."

We went back to getting dinner ready. Cliff started slicing up sausage for the jambalaya we were making, and I pulled out a pot to start boiling water for the rice. But then I realized something. I looked over at Cliff.

"You don't have to go, do you?"

Cliff looked back at me and raised his eyebrows. His sheepish grin told me I was right.

Busted.

"You don't have to go, but you want to go," I gently accused. "Because you just got back from the other deployment, you don't technically have to go on this one."

I grabbed a dish towel and swatted playfully at him, pushing him back against the counter and giving him a little kiss. "That's right, I'm a military spouse. I'm a *smart* military spouse."

He smiled and chuckled, knowing he'd been caught.

I turned back to what I was doing. He didn't have to go, but I knew there was no way he would say no, not when his whole battalion was going. None of the others who had already deployed with him would say no either. There was a duty there, a sense of honor, a code you didn't break. You trained together, you deployed together. That's just the way it was.

I wouldn't expect anything less.

I've noticed lately that Cliff is getting louder. And it's getting on my nerves. When we discuss things like bills or finances or Caleb or anything else he knows is important, his volume level goes up. I wonder if this is his way of being more assertive. I don't like it. I really don't like it. And now I'm worried I've opened a box I can no longer close.

The other night I tried talking to him yet again about this overwhelming pressure I feel about trying to do it all. I guess I'd define *all* as everything—managing the house, the son, the chores, the meals, and all the other responsibilities that come with my job and my ministry—freelance writing, book writing, speaking, trying to move my military wives ministry toward being more organized and established. My dream to offer encouraging weekends for wives going through deployment. It's a lot to keep a handle on, and most of the time I feel like I'm failing. Some days I just want an "off" button to push.

"Look, you're doing fine, you just need to get better organized," he said as we lay there in our bed.

I don't know why we always pick this time of day to have these talks, but we do. And this one wasn't going well. His tone was louder, again, and he seemed a lot more aggressive in the way he was talking to me. He was basically saying I needed to suck it up and carry on. Maybe he was right, but I didn't like being treated like one of his subordinates in his unit.

"If you think it's so easy, then you tell me how to do that, Cliff."

I rolled over as I turned the light off and stewed in the dark. I felt overwhelmed with no clear answers on how to better manage everything. And him being loud wasn't solving any of it.

The next morning, he stopped me in the hallway as I was walking back toward our room after dropping Caleb off at school.

"I'm calling for our hug," he said.

I hate it when he does this. Because he usually does it when I'm mad. Which is why he does it, and which is why, deep down, I'm grateful for the husband God knew I needed.

The rule is we hug for twenty seconds. And usually by the end, whatever either of us was upset about has melted away. It's a good way for us to remind ourselves of what truly matters. And it usually ends in kisses.

This time was no exception. Cliff kissed me and started leading me backward toward our room. As he walked me back, my eyes closed, my arms around his neck, I couldn't help but think, *Can he take the lead? Can I let him take the lead? Are we trying to fix what isn't broken?*

For Mother's Day, Cliff told me to stay in bed and relax while he and Caleb made me breakfast. An omelet with bacon and orange juice. Caleb was so sweet as he walked in, holding the tray. Cliff was right behind him. As Caleb walked it over to my bed and said "Happy Mother's Day, Mom!" he stumbled, and the plate slid down the tray. Cliff managed to grab it before it spilled all over the comforter. Whew.

While I enjoyed my breakfast, I read through an article that was floating around Facebook and Twitter about how far women have come and how far we have to go. I have been one of those women who felt frustrated juggling a full-time job with being a mom and wife and managing a home. The article was by a woman who had held a prominent government position and had stepped down specifically to spend more time with her sons before they grew up and went to college. As I read through it, I was hopeful she would explain why that was so important to her. Instead, she wrote mostly about the structure of work in America not being flexible enough for women, and the only way it will ever get that way is if more and more women put themselves into higher positions of power in order to change the rules.

I'm not so sure that's really the answer.

When I started this experiment, I didn't do it with the idea that I would follow a complementarian viewpoint or an egalitarian viewpoint. I just wanted to investigate what the Bible said and try to follow it. I think labels can sometimes cause problems rather than be helpful because each woman who is a wife and a mom has her own situations and challenges she deals with. So to fit completely into one box or the other, one viewpoint or another, doesn't always work. But to follow and apply what Scripture says to our lives should be our priority. That's what I want my priority to be.

I don't think I would ever say all women should stay home, or all women need to work outside their homes, or all couples need to be equal in everything. But I do believe God made men and women different, and he did so because those differences complement one another. And when we ignore those differences and insist that we're all the same, I wonder how much of a blessing we're missing out on. Instead of fighting the differences, as I have done for a long time, what if we stepped back and decided to enjoy the differences and celebrate the differences and accept that those differences are what makes each of us unique? And that it's good?

As a woman, I do believe I need my husband. And as a man, I believe my husband needs me. I think about two women I know, two acquaintances. These women are bloggers who met online a few years ago and almost overnight became best friends. They do everything together—travel back and forth to each other's houses, talk for hours on the phone, help with each other's kids (there's six kids between them). I've followed them on their blogs and on Facebook. But recently, I learned both of them are divorcing their husbands and they're moving in together. And I suspect they've fallen in love with each other. These women were extremely committed Christians who loved God's Word and loved their husbands. But somewhere along the way, they became convinced they no longer needed their husbands because they had each other.

Doesn't it go back to what God wants versus what I want? Doesn't it come down to following God's Word because I believe it to be the authority over my life? Maybe submission is a reminder to both husbands and wives that it's not about us. It's about God. It's about service to him. Honor to him. That this is not some form of old-fashioned twisted slavery but praise and honor and recognition to the One who created us. The One who loves us. Who cares for us.

I've been studying James 4:7-10 lately, and I'm struck over and over by what it says:

> Therefore, submit to God. But resist the Devil, and he will
> flee from you. Draw near to God, and He will draw near

to you. Cleanse your hands, sinners, and purify your hearts, double-minded people! Be miserable and mourn and weep. Your laughter must change to mourning and your joy to sorrow. Humble yourselves before the Lord, and He will exalt you.

In this passage, James gave out ten commands needed to resolve conflict among believers, and they came with conditions. If you do X, then Y will happen. Submit to God. Resist the Devil, resist temptation, and it will leave you. Draw closer to God and he'll draw closer to you. Humble yourself before God and he will lift you up.

Can I ever get to a place in my marriage where I see the relationship with my husband as holy because we were brought together by a holy God? And that honoring my husband and being intentional in how I treat him, selflessly and to the best of my ability, is one way to also honor and be intentional in how I serve God? Not honoring my husband as if *he* is God, but honoring him because God has placed him in my life, and God's Word says I should. And God also has instructions and directions for how my husband should honor me.

I may not feel like going to buy groceries today, but I go anyway. And isn't that the point? We die to ourselves in order to serve God in whatever situation he's called us? Even in the cereal aisle?

Dr. Mom Meets Dr. Wife

Caleb has been sick with the flu for a week. His fever started on Sunday night, right before the last two days of his fifth grade year. It was an odd time of year to get the flu, but the flu test came back positive. His doctor said lots of liquids and lots of rest. Well, at least for one of us.

By Caleb's second day of being sick, I wasn't feeling very well myself. Aches and chills were coming and going, and I was very, very tired. Caleb was waking up about every three hours to throw up, usually when his medicine wore off and his temperature spiked again. Normally he was pretty good about getting up and making it to the bathroom in time, but this bout of flu was tough, and I was changing sheets and giving medicine at all hours of the day and night, while still trying to keep the house picked up and dinner on the table each night.

By the time Wednesday rolled around, I was exhausted. Cliff walked in that night after a meeting that ran late and found both Caleb and me sitting on the couch, watching TV. Well, Caleb was; I was just too tired to move. I didn't say much after Cliff got home, but I wanted him to say something. After I got Caleb to bed a little early, I came back into the living room. Cliff was sitting on the far couch, playing a game on his iPad. I sat down on the other, blankly watching the TV screen, but inside my head, I was really yelling for Cliff to speak. I wanted him to tell me the house looked good despite the fact I'd played Nurse Nightingale for seventy-two hours straight. Tell me I've done great and you appreciate how I've cared for our son. But I didn't get anything. He just sat, his eyes glued to his iPad, while I tried to keep my eyes even open.

When we finally headed to bed and turned out the lights, I worked up the nerve to talk to him. I rolled over toward him in the dark. I couldn't see his face, but I knew he was still awake.

"You know," I started, "it would really have meant a lot if you'd said something tonight about how I've done this week taking care of Caleb and the house and dinner and all."

"I'm sorry," he said, his tone sounding defensive. "I guess it would have been nice if you had told me you were happy to see *me*."

I lay there in the dark, my mouth hanging open. I couldn't believe it.

Seriously? I'm knee-deep in vomit-stained laundry, working on four hours of sleep so he could have his rest to go to work, and he's upset that I don't do the June Cleaver thing and greet him at the door? I was flummoxed.

"You know what?" I said. "You're being really selfish."

Sometimes helpers need to help their heads of household know when they're wrong. I rolled over and stared angrily into the darkness. If being a helper means being treated this way, no thanks. All bets were quite off and this experiment was about to get dumped.

He apologized the next morning. And so did I. After some time to think about it, I saw how my attention was so focused on Caleb that, right or wrong, Cliff may have just felt left out. So Thursday night when he came home, I made a point to smile and give him a hug and tell him I was glad to see him. There was a good dinner ready to be eaten, and I even made a point to throw a pretty bright-red tablecloth on the table. Just like you don't get time off from being a mom, maybe you also don't get time off from being a wife. He still needs me too.

It's easy sometimes to spend all our time as moms focused on our kids. They need us so much more readily. But our marriages need us to make them priorities. Our husbands do too.

Honor on the Wall

I've been going through some of the last holdovers of boxes in the garage to organize, mostly of Cliff's navy stuff, and I ran across a special plaque that recognized Cliff as "Junior Sailor of the Quarter" back many, many years ago. I brought it into our room and sat on our bed and looked at it for a long time.

The year he received this was one of the busiest of our marriage. I remember when he came home and told me. He probably wouldn't have, but he was carrying it in his hand and I happened to notice. He had made it out to be lot less of a big deal than it actually was. That was around the same time I'd traveled overseas to report on the Iraq War, and the more I sat there and looked at that plaque, dated around the same time I'd traveled, the more I realized I'd missed celebrating my husband's accomplishment. And he had supported me in my endeavors. He had encouraged me. He'd celebrated my success back then. He'd kept his out of the spotlight. At the time, I was so fixed on my own travels and my own success that I hadn't done anything for him.

A wave of sadness and guilt washed over me. I hadn't honored him. I hadn't been intentional about helping him back then. And I was definitely the most selfish person I knew. But I could do what I could to right the wrong now.

I found a nail and I hung his plaque in a prominent place on the wall next to his closet. Where he could see it every time he went by there and could remember his accomplishment. And I could too.

He noticed a couple of days later. I explained to him that it should have been hung a long time before now. I think in some ways he thought it was probably silly, but he never asked me to take it down.

That night, as we were cleaning up after dinner, Cliff walked over to the desk in the kitchen and picked up the devotional I'd bought about two months earlier and started flipping through it.

"Want to start this tonight?" he asked.

"Uh, yeah, that would be nice," I said, surprised but excited.

That night we came together as a family for the first time, and Cliff led us through a devotional reading. Caleb had his iPad and excitedly looked up Scriptures Cliff called out. And then we prayed together and went over what the rest of the week looked like for each of us.

I don't know whether my little way of honoring Cliff this week by putting that plaque up had anything to do with him deciding to start our family devotions together. But I'd like to think—no, I have to believe—that just as God is working on my heart for change, for perhaps some new perspective with this whole submission and stepping back business, that he's also working on Cliff's heart as head of household. As I step back and let my husband have the room to step forward and lead as God has called him to lead, maybe, just maybe, I'm going to see other changes in Cliff.

Fifty Shades of Distraction

School is out, Caleb's back to being healthy, and summer has started, which means Cliff's busy season of travel for work has also begun. In the next forty-five days, he'll be gone for thirty, mostly during the week and home on weekends. Part of that time, though, will be his annual two-week training for the navy. I've tried to approach this season as "it is what it is," and make the best of it. And there's no way I will complain because 1) I'm grateful he has a job at all, the way the economy is, and 2) I'm grateful that job helps pay for this house.

I'm keeping myself busy with freelance assignments, book writing, and preventing Caleb from sitting in front of the television all day every day. One downside to having an only child is it's harder to say "just go outside" if he's going to be by himself the whole time. The kids around this neighborhood seem to play in backyards if they're outside playing at all, and most of them are younger. He does have one very good friend his age, the daughter of our good friends who live about a five-minute walk from our house. She's an only kid too. So they get together at least a couple of times a week, riding bikes and playing at each of our homes.

A new book series has come out that has taken women, and the world, by storm. The first book in the trilogy is called *Fifty Shades of Grey* and it's categorized as erotic fiction. I didn't pay much attention to it. Though I don't think I've ever read anything as steamy, I did read the occasional romance novel as a teenager and a college student. But I stopped reading those after I got married. I thought the real thing was so much better.

What's surprised me about this new series isn't that it's wildly popular and a bestseller—sex always sells—but it's surprising that a lot of Christian women are reading it and raving about it. I'm the first person to say don't criticize something unless you've read it first, but this is one of those situations where I don't think it does any good to read it first—not with the risk of graphic images sticking with you afterwards.

I remember reading the V.C. Andrews books when I was in middle school. Those were extremely popular. *Flowers in the Attic. Petals on the Wind.* Girls in my class (including me) did book reports on these books, which had detailed sexual acts written all through them, including examples of incest. We did book reports. Seriously. We were eighth graders and sharing these in class. (For the record, I'm pretty sure the boys in those days thought we were nuts.) I can't imagine what our parents or our teachers were thinking. I can still remember a couple of scenes if I think about it—and no, they're not examples of the wonderful plot or sweet romance.

Countless studies have shown what pornography does to people who are exposed to it over and over, and I personally know of situations where pornography has destroyed a life and destroyed a family. It's caused havoc in the lives of men. Why would we want to open the door in our lives as women? As wives? As moms?

We may not be holding a magazine filled with pictures of nude men in our hands, and many women say they're reading these books just for the love story. But isn't that similar to what men say about their magazines? They aren't really looking at the pictures; they just read the articles? So we can ignore the visual images those words on the page produce in our minds? As someone who spends a lot of time choosing words that will help readers connect visually to what I've written, I highly doubt that.

If we are servants of God, if we identify ourselves the way James does as literally "a slave of God and of the Lord Jesus Christ" (1:1), if we want to follow God and not ourselves, I think we need to stop and think about what God says about sex in contrast to what the world says:

> Now the works of the flesh are obvious: sexual immorality, moral impurity, promiscuity, idolatry, sorcery, hatreds, strife, jealousy, outbursts of anger, selfish ambitions, dissensions, factions, envy, drunkenness, carousing, and anything similar. I tell you about these things in advance—as I told you before—that those who practice such things will not inherit the kingdom of God (Galatians 5:19-21).

Do not be wise in your own eyes;
    fear the Lord and shun evil.
This will bring health to your body
    and nourishment to your bones.

(Proverbs 3:7-8 NIV)

Finally, brothers and sisters, whatever is true, whatever is noble, whatever is right, whatever is pure, whatever is lovely, whatever is admirable—if anything is excellent or praiseworthy—think about such things (Philippians 4:8 NIV).

So I'm wondering: how many of us are really following Eve instead of following Jesus?

Desiring what we want?

Ignoring what God says?

Choosing to believe there will be no consequences from our choices?

The interesting thing about this book series is that it's all about submission. A woman being controlled sexually by a man. Not for her good. But for his pleasure. And I guess in some weird way she's supposed to get pleasure from that as well. It's what the world tells us is good for us.

But that's not how God describes sex in the Bible. In Ephesians, husbands are told to "love their wives as their own bodies...for no one ever hates his own flesh, but provides and cares for it, just as Christ does for the church" (5:28-29). Husbands love their wives, they don't hold them down and do things to them because they enjoy being in control. That is a twisted sense of love.

So it confuses me that women who follow Christ want to follow this set of stories. Following God's commands means leaving our wishes behind. We can convince ourselves all we want that it's OK, that it's the story we care about, that reading about two other people having sex will only make our own marital relationships better. Really? God isn't out to make us unhappy, but he does want us holy before he wants us happy. He created us to love him, follow him, serve him. He didn't create us to do what we want and expect him to just be OK with it.

Serving God means following what he says. Even when we don't like it. If we struggle with something as small as what to watch or what to read, how do we know we'll hold fast to what he says in the harder stuff? When we're tempted to cheat on our spouses? When we're tempted to steal from a friend? Or lie to save ourselves from embarrassment or trouble?

What God says, he means. But so many of us don't know what he says. We need to read his Word. Not take the word of other people who read it, but read it for ourselves.

I got mad two years ago when my pastor preached on the Proverbs 31 wife. I was tempted to write off what he said. But I chose not to ignore my anger, and I asked God to show me what he wanted me to learn. And he did. And I can tell you that two years later, I am more at peace than I have ever been. And my family is happier for it too. And just so it is said—because it always seems to come up as an argument that people who shoot down books and movies about sex must not like sex very much—my husband and I have an amazing marriage and sex life. I am seriously blessed, and very happy.

Fifty Shades of Grey is just a book. There have been similar books before it and there will be similar books after it. *Magic Mike* is just another movie. They weren't written or produced for Christians, they weren't written for believers. But they're being read and viewed by Christians. And I think these are only symptoms of a much bigger issue.

Do we follow God or do we follow ourselves?

Think about it.

If we're just following ourselves—if we ask for God's help only when we want it and we ignore the rest of what he says—we don't really have a relationship with Christ. We just have a bunch of rules we've made up and pretend to follow until we don't want to. But a relationship with Christ means giving all of myself.

It's hard. It's messy. But it's worth it. Because the joy I get from following him, the love I feel from knowing him, is a whole lot better than anything I might gain from some erotic novel. Or watching a bunch of half-nude guys dancing around for two hours. That stuff leaves quick, and what's left is emptiness. But Jesus doesn't leave.

Serving God isn't easy. But he loves us. Unconditionally. Relentlessly. And it's not that hard to serve someone who loves you. Knowing him and serving him makes things much more clear. When we get caught up in distractions such as a steamy novel series, it takes us away from what truly matters—focusing on and pursuing what God desires for us.

Speaking of distractions, I had a major one the other night. Cliff was gone, and I had just started boiling some chicken for dinner when my mom called. She has started helping out the Horns by spending nights and weekends with Mamaw when they travel, and she and Mamaw were going out to dinner and did we want to join them?

I hurriedly turned off the boiling chicken, but as I was dashing out of the kitchen to go throw on some decent clothes and makeup, I turned the burner back on because the chicken just didn't look quite done yet.

We were halfway to the restaurant when I had the nagging thought, *Did I turn the stove off?* I normally have this thought whenever I leave the house, even if I haven't cooked in six hours. Cliff is usually with me, and we'll turn around and drive back, I'll get out of the car, unlock the door, go check, and yes, everything is off and I've just wasted ten minutes of our time and made us late.

This time I decided I wouldn't listen to my little guilt-ridden conscience. I was (semi-sure) I'd turned the burner off. But sitting in the restaurant with Mom and Mamaw, I still wasn't convinced. I even joked that I probably shouldn't stay very long in case my house was burning down. An hour and twenty minutes later, we finally made our way back home.

And walked into a kitchen full of white smoke.

"Whoa!" Caleb exclaimed.

I went to the stove and quickly turned off the burner.

The water in the pot had completely evaporated, and the chicken was sitting there, surrounded by a charred mess. I poked at the chicken, which was actually a rather nice golden brown, and it flaked off tenderly. If it weren't for the black soot and ash surrounding it, it would probably be delicious.

I quickly moved the pot over to the sink, then ran around to open all our windows, wondering what the neighbors might think. That's when I realized something. There was no loud annoying sound blaring. Where was the smoke alarm?

I looked up. No smoke alarm in the kitchen. Huh. That was odd.

I walked into the game room. Nope, nothing there. Living room. Nope. Spare bedroom. Negative. Caleb's room, the hall, our room.

We'd lived in this house for four months and not once did we realize there were no smoke alarms.

I called Cliff. "Hey, did you know we don't have any smoke alarms in this house?"

"Really?" he said, stretched out in his hotel room after a long day of telling teachers how little they had to retire on.

"Yes, and would you like to know how I know?"

"Uh, yeeesss?" he said.

"I almost burned down the house with chicken."

"Huh. Really."

"Yes. Can you take care of putting smoke alarms in when you get home this weekend, please?"

"Yes, I can do that. And I'm glad you're OK."

"Thanks. Me too."

Cliff came home on Friday and kept his promise. He installed smoke detectors in our kitchen and all of the bedrooms. I wonder if it might be smart to add one in the hall too. But I'm trying to show respect and honor to my husband. Besides, that area of the house isn't exactly spread out, so I guess we'll be OK.

The kitchen, though, I'm not so sure. Cliff installed the alarm right over the central area where the stove and oven are. There's a problem with that. And we found out the next time I put something in the oven. The alarm went off when I opened the oven door. Just the little wave of heat coming out of the oven was enough to set off the alarm. The loud, obnoxious alarm. The only way to prevent it from going off is to turn on the fan. The tacky brass fan hanging in the middle of the kitchen that I originally thought we might remove altogether.

Looks like the fan is staying. Because my "once it's there, I'm not moving it" husband isn't moving the smoke alarm.

I have a feeling there will be a lot of false alarms in our future.

Little Surprises

We are getting used to Cliff being gone. OK, that's what I'm supposed to say. But honestly, after the second week of seeing him less than our dog, the absence wears a little thin. I feel like I'm on an endless loop of dinner and laundry with no break in sight. With Caleb home and no school routine to fall on, it gets a little tougher.

Cliff comes home for one night or a couple days, happy and energized to be back, and I feel like death warmed over and like we're living two different lives. It's hard not to feel a little resentful of his "hotel living, restaurant meal indulging, and bringing home the laundry for the little wifey to do so he can leave again" lifestyle.

But I'm supposed to be intentional in being his helper, right? So I shake off the crabbiness and I focus on what we have coming up next. Dinner with his parents.

Since we moved into the house, we haven't seen a whole lot of the Horns. They still have a full travel schedule of trips Ms. Nancy leads as a tour guide for the travel agency. My mom stays with Mamaw when they're away, though Mom works during the day, so she's only at the house at night and a little on weekends. We've had the occasional lunch after church with them and the rest of the family, but mostly we've spent time working on the house and making sure we're bringing in the income to pay our bills. It still feels like an uphill climb in many ways, but we're taking it one step at a time.

Until just last week, we'd been eating at the small four-seater table we'd borrowed from the Horns until we could get a new dining room set. But Cliff and I finally were able to look for a table last week, and after visiting four different stores, we agreed on the table we had liked at the very first store. Now we have an eight-foot table with six real chairs to seat folks. Ten if we bring the portable chairs in and everyone crowds around. It's time to invite people over.

Ms. Nancy and Mr. Ray weren't home for Father's Day, which was a couple of weeks ago, so I thought it would be nice to have them over for dinner so we could at least catch up. I decided to keep the meal simple, so with Cliff's blessing, I breaded and baked some chicken tenderloins and cooked green beans and mashed potatoes with gravy. I scrubbed the house spotless, and put a pretty white tablecloth out.

It's hard not to get antsy and worry about what Ms. Nancy thinks. My eyes can already spot a whole lot she'll notice isn't right. The out-of-date brass light fixtures and fans. The tacky brass knobs on all the kitchen cabinets. I'm trying to ignore the big scratch across the tile under the dining room table. But that's what happens when you buy a house that has to get sold. There's usually a whole lot that needs to be fixed. And we'll get there. In a few years.

I'd stressed about the food getting done in time and almost worried Cliff to death. But the Horns didn't arrive until after I'd taken the chicken out of the oven, and of course I'd forgotten to turn the fan on. Score one more for the smoke alarm. I turned the fan on and refused to silently swear against my husband. When our guests walked in, I welcomed Mamaw with a big hug and helped her carefully find a chair at the table. I gave Ms. Nancy and Mr. Ray both a hug as Ms. Nancy put her purse down on the counter and asked if she could help with anything. I told her it was all ready to go.

I always feel self-conscious when it comes to inviting people over. Hospitality has never felt like a gift of mine. In Tennessee, I once went to visit an older military wife—someone I looked up to greatly. We sat down in her living room, and she brought out this cute little tray with a beautiful and dainty teapot with little sugar and cream bowls. I barely remember what we talked about because I was so impressed by the cute little setup, and I spent the entire time wondering why I didn't know how to do that.

I put on my best smile and asked Cliff to get drinks and tried to be conversational. I asked Ms. Nancy how their most recent trip was, and she quickly went into her storytelling mode of how beautiful everything was and how great all her travelers were, and I let her talk while I got the bread out and buttered.

"So when are you changing *that* out?" she asked as she stared up at the ugly brass chandelier hanging over the table.

"I know, I know, it's ugly," I said, as I brought some napkins (or paper towels folded up like napkins) over to the table and everyone started sitting down. I took my seat next to Cliff and tried not to think about all the priorities we had right now for our limited funds that included more of the basics such as electricity, food, and gas. We're also trying to save for a second car since right now we're borrowing one of the Horns' cars because they're rarely home to use it. "Someday."

Everyone ate quietly, and except for a little small talk between Mr. Ray and Cliff about the shop and plans for what he was going to put in there one day, there wasn't a whole lot of other conversation. I asked Mamaw how she was feeling and what she was up to. She'd read the newspaper that morning and took a nap that afternoon. Good to know.

No one said anything about the food. Not even Cliff. This drove me a little crazy on the inside. I thought about kicking him to get his attention, but I didn't. That would definitely not be submissive. I mean, it wasn't a horrible meal. I don't even think it was anywhere close to being one of my top ten bad meals. It was a good meal.

But it was quiet from everyone until dessert time.

I brought out the key lime pie I'd bought, knowing Mr. Ray and Cliff both like it. I'd barely passed the plates and forks around, and the compliments just started pouring out.

"Oh, wow, this is great."

"Really good."

"Sara, this pie is mighty tasty." (That was from Mamaw.)

Of course it was. It was straight out of the box.

On Friday, I had just started looking at what I might fix for dinner and was about to empty the dishwasher when in walked Cliff. It was three thirty in the afternoon, and he had come home early. He was carrying flowers.

Oh. My. Word. He could have asked me to scrub the floor with a toothbrush at that moment, and I would have done it. OK, maybe not with a toothbrush, but I would have cleaned it with something.

Bring me flowers and you bring me joy. And it's not even the flowers that make me happy, because this girl has no green thumbs. The only flowers I can identify with confidence are roses, tulips (because they're my favorite), and dead ones. Because that's usually how they end up in my care.

It's the thought that wows me so much. Cliff and I once took the test for finding out what your love languages are. Mine is Words and Acts of Service. Cliff's is Physical Touch and Acts of Service. Both of us score the lowest on Gifts. I would much rather you do something for me or tell me something encouraging than buy me something. But bringing me flowers tells me without a doubt that I am loved. Not because of the money that was spent—you could bring me wild daisies from the park and I'd feel like a princess—but for the time and the action you took to do it.

Cliff pulled me in close and gave me a big kiss. "I know you've been working hard while I've been out of town so much, and I just wanted you to know how much I appreciate you and how much I love you. Now go sit down and I'll handle the dishes."

I didn't go sit down, but I did sit at the counter in the kitchen and talked to him while he worked. Basking in a love tank now full.

A week later we were back in the kitchen, working on another meal. Except not a full meal this time, since it's for our small group at church, which is holding its quarterly "Dinner for Six." One couple hosts the dinner at their house, and then two other couples, randomly picked from our class coordinator, bring sides or whatever else is needed. It's a good time to get to know each other better and have some fellowship.

These types of dinners always make me nervous, though I've gained a little more confidence in the kitchen since my Proverbs 31 experiment. The couple hosting the dinner is planning on barbecue pork as the main dish, and the rest of us will bring sides. Fred, the husband of the pair, is actually the one planning everything because as his wife Julie proudly admits, he cooks a whole lot better. So I texted him to make sure potato salad was good. I'd asked earlier whether he wanted potato salad or baked beans, and he had said either sounded fine.

"Weren't you going to do something else too?" he texted back.

Oh great. I guess I can do both.

"Sure!" I texted back. "Be happy to."

I had an hour and a half to cook two dishes, two dishes I might add that I was cooking from scratch. Well, almost.

I used fresh cubed potatoes for the potato salad, and though I used cans for the baked beans, I had learned enough from Cliff and the Pioneer Woman's website to doctor it up. The Pioneer Woman suggested bacon, which I layered all the way across the top of the baked beans and stuck in the oven to cook. That was going to be good.

But still I was sweating it. We had a lot to get done and not a lot of time. I asked Cliff to help me by chopping up some onions and boiled eggs for the potato salad. As we worked together, I had flashbacks of the small group dinner we'd tried to work together on when we had lived in Anderson, back during the Proverbs 31 experiment. That one hadn't gone so well. I'd become very offended when I felt like he'd taken over.

Today was different though. We worked as a team. I was happy, doing my thing. He was helping and not telling me how something should be done that I wasn't doing right. Maybe my cooking skills had improved. Or maybe we'd just learned how to flow a little better as a couple. Whatever the reason, it felt really good. And the food smelled great.

We made it to our friends' house on time and enjoyed getting to visit. After dinner, I took Cliff's plate and cleaned his place at the table for him, while he talked with the guys. I grabbed his cup and brought him a refill of sweet tea. As I sat back down, it dawned on me, as everyone chatted away, that I'd been the only one to do that. The other guys had gotten up and served themselves. The wives hadn't seemed to pay attention nor offered their husbands anything when they got up.

I felt a little bit freakish on the inside. Was I that weird now? Waiting on my husband? But I liked being sweet and looking out for him, even in those small ways. Doing something thoughtful for him didn't seem so wrong, even if it did make me feel a little like an oddball compared to everyone else.

What was this experiment doing to me?

Heather and her husband, Andre, came over the other night with their little boy for pizza and to tackle a very important project that the guys, I'm sure, were still scratching their heads over.

We were making liquid laundry detergent.

In my quest to be helper and find ways to make our budget breathe a little easier, I'd found a homemade detergent recipe on Pinterest. Julie, the girl whose house we'd gone to the other night, had used it for months and loved it. So I knew we had to try it.

After dinner, their son and Caleb went into the game room while Heather and I got to work making our special detergent. Neither of us consider ourselves to be homemakers in the traditional sense of the word, though I think we both try to provide good homes for our families. Heather works a full-time marketing job at the hospital in town. We're both all about saving money, and so we were curious to see if this homemade detergent works. With Julie offering a first-person testimony, I thought we didn't have much to lose.

I'd bought all the ingredients we needed from Walmart—borax, washing soda, Fels-Naptha soap bars—and I'd told Heather to be sure to bring a five-gallon bucket with a lid.

The guys sat at the table and talked while we girls started grating the soap bars. We had to add hot water and the soap flakes to a pot on the stove. Cliff and Andre enjoyed teasing us a bit as we took turns stirring, and Heather and I couldn't help but laugh at the sight of us stirring soap, of all things.

But the guys soon changed their tone.

When it came time to mix all the ingredients together in the bucket, we added more hot water, the soap mixture, and then the borax and washing soda. We needed the guys' help carrying the bucket to where it would sit overnight, and according to the recipe, the detergent would look like gel the next day. We'd have to stir it up really good again, and then we could use it.

Cliff read over the instructions to Andre as we started the next batch. "Hey, you actually add water to what you put in the detergent bottle," he said.

"I know," I said, as I gave him a smile. "One cent a load."

The guys did the math and realized that the five-gallon bucket we were filling would produce ten gallons of laundry detergent. They looked at each other.

"We need to find a recipe for dish detergent," Andre said.

Who's Got the Authority?

This morning I woke up at my usual time, a little before five, and got up and started moving before I had to wake Caleb at six. This is one of my favorite times of the day, next to our times at night when we still read and pray together and I tuck him in. Since he's eleven now, I keep thinking that it's going to end soon, the ticktock of the clock of childhood may not be sounding much longer. I keep waiting for the day he rolls his eyes at me as I try to stretch out on his bed with him to read one more chapter, and he says, "Mom, I got this."

But for the moment, he's still my little boy, and until he does kick me out, I will still read and kiss him good night and wake him up in the mornings. He is easy when it comes to waking up. He doesn't groan or whine or complain. Most of the time he wakes up with a smile. And even when he's tired, he'll simply nicely whisper, with his eyes still closed and his hands pulling the covers up to his chin, "Can I have just five more minutes?"

This morning, though, he seemed to have something serious on his mind.

"Mom," he said, sitting up and leaning back against the wall behind his bed, "can I talk to you about something?"

I sat next to him. "Sure, what's up?"

"Last night I asked Dad if I could get a video game for my iPad, and he said no. Can you talk to him?"

I could hear the emergency alert system in my brain before Caleb's question even finished.

This is a test. This is a test of the Emergency Parenting System. Will you recognize your husband's authority as father? Or will you step in and usurp with your own authority as mother? This is a test…

My first instinct was to be the good guy, the mom who tsk-tsks about how cruel and horrible Father is and, using my sweet charms, says, "Oh, don't you worry, honey. I'll talk to him for you." Or even better, tells him to just go ahead and get it. That would score me huge mama points.

There were so many years when Caleb was little that I'd always felt like the bad guy—the disciplinarian, the one who said no. Dad was the fun one, the parent who didn't say no, the cool dad who cracked jokes instead of orders to go brush teeth, the buddy who liked playing games and didn't do all that boring stuff like cleaning the kitchen and making the beds. And usually he was the one who said yes, if he wasn't saying, "Go ask your mom."

But lately, Cliff was saying no. I was seeing him take more of a lead in parenting Caleb, or maybe he was just playing a more active part. He wasn't saying "go ask your mom" as much. He was making more decisions on his own with Caleb. Sometimes he'd come ask me what I thought. He was leading our family devotionals each week, he was asking Caleb questions about God, starting discussions about God. He was being the head of our household.

I had a choice. I could be Mom or I could support Dad. I went back to that verse in Ephesians, "Wives, understand and support your husbands in ways that show your support for Christ" (5:22 MSG).

I took a breath.

"Well, why did Dad say no?" I asked Caleb, thinking I could walk him through his conversation with Cliff so he might understand better.

"Because he thought it was really expensive, and I needed to save my money. He told me I needed to wait, and if I wanted it in a few weeks, to talk to him again."

"OK, what do you think about that?"

"I think I want the game *now*," Caleb said, looking at me with this *hello!* expression on his face.

"OK, well, let me ask you another question," I said. "Does your dad love you and want the best for you?"

Caleb's lips formed a pout. "Yes."

"Do you think he's just wanting to be mean and not let you have the game?"

Caleb sighed and tried not rolling his eyes as he looked up at the ceiling. "No."

"OK, then. Listen to Dad. If you still really want the game in a couple of weeks, go back and talk to him. But remember that his decision is the decision we go with."

Caleb wasn't happy as he trudged down the hall to the bathroom to get ready for school—who is when we don't get what we really want?—but he agreed to my suggestion. He's learning what it means to wait for what he wants.

And maybe, just maybe, I'm learning something too.

Do Submissive Wives Stay Home?

've come to a realization these last few months that we've lived in our house.

I need to do a better job at bringing in income. But I'm struggling with this one. Because I'm not so good at the balance thing. When I'm focused on our house and on meals and on keeping laundry done and clean clothes in the closet, I'm actually pretty good at it—now. I've learned a lot. I've gotten better at some things. When I'm in my office, working on a new writing project, or planning and dreaming with my military wives leadership team, or redesigning a website, I can focus along with the best of them and get things done.

But when I try to put both together—managing home and work—it's like trying to speak Chinese in France. Because I have never learned Chinese and I have never been to France. So everything slows waaaaay down.

That's how I feel right now as I try to navigate this submissive wife experiment. I'm not interested in what everyone else is doing because, as I wrote during my Proverbs 31 experiment, I believe each wife and mom has to figure out through the circumstances and experiences God gives her how his Word applies to her specific situation. But I am interested in figuring out how I can be submissive to my husband and still be a passionate professional. How can I work and stay focused on work and still be a helper to Cliff? Is it even possible?

I came across a blog post a wife wrote recently that told the story of how she had been involved in a private Facebook group with some other Christian wives. She'd become pretty discouraged at the reaction of the group when another member announced she was going to have to go back to work. Her husband needed her to; income was tight. This group of women started fussing at her for even considering getting a job, and they'd berated her husband for not being willing to do "whatever it took," which meant getting an extra two or three jobs to support his family. The blogger who wrote about this was bewildered at the reaction and dismayed at how other women could be so quick to pass judgment.

So it makes me wonder: Does being a submissive wife mean being a lazy wife? Or put nicer, does it mean we're entitled to being princesses in our king's castles? Do we really think God's plan is for husbands to work themselves to death? I don't think so.

I think about Cliff and what he's doing for us. He's working a job that isn't necessarily his favorite, but it pays our bills, though the comfort margin isn't great. He also serves in the military. Since I was actually the bigger breadwinner when we first married, is it really fair for me to now step back and say, "OK, hon, it's all up you to bring home the bacon. Get to it."

I'm getting the hang of this housekeeping thing. Cliff hasn't touched laundry in over two months, which he was nice enough to mention yesterday after he got home from work and I probably too eagerly replied, "Yes, I know."

We have no debt except our house. But a state job doesn't exactly provide the income to set up a family for life. So I'm struggling with making the bread and helping the breadwinner bring in the bread.

My type A personality wants me to take on the challenge, like an over-eager cheerleader with a big "we're number one" foam finger on my hand, screaming "We're in it to win it!" and stop at nothing until we reach our goal. But Cliff isn't exactly like that. He doesn't get worked up. He doesn't race ahead. He takes one day at a time. And that's enough. If we were on a racecourse, I would be the rabbit and he would be the turtle. He would still reach the finish line, just like me, but probably not be worn out when he got there.

So what does the Bible say? When I look into the verses about submission, I see references to women taking care of the home, but I don't see anything that says women should always stay at home. When I look at other parts of the Bible, I also see examples of women who had responsibilities outside the family.

I don't want to run or get ahead of my husband. So maybe it's easier to say that it's his job to bring income in, but it's my job to manage it. To not be so concerned about bringing the bacon in as much as what to do with it after we have it. I've tried this, to a point, and it's helping.

Once a month, I go to Sam's to buy our meat in bulk, and I come home and divide it into gallon and quart-size bags to freeze. I also take snacks, like cheese crackers or cookies or popcorn, and divide those into one-serving size or smaller bags that Caleb can just grab when he gets hungry. Last night I did this, and I caught Cliff standing at the doorway between the kitchen and the living room watching me.

"What are you looking at?" I asked, as I picked up a third chicken breast to add to a quart-size bag.

"I love it when you do that," he said.

I rolled my eyes. He walked over to the counter.

"No, seriously, I just think it's neat. I like the way you take care of us like this."

It made me feel good to feel appreciated, but I still think I need to be doing more in the income area. Our problem isn't spending. It's just making enough to keep going.

But how can I be assertive and submissive at the same time? It seems like such a matter of opposites. And yet, I think about some of the women I know who are leaders in their organizations. One woman just recently became vice president of a Christian corporation and president of her division. She's also one of the sweetest, most compassionate women I know. She loves Jesus and loves her husband and her family and is devoted to what the Bible says. I wonder if she's found the secret to being both assertive and submissive? I suspect she has.

So this morning, I talked to Cliff about some things I want to do with my websites and some software I want to buy. I've gone a couple of years now, through all the craziness of our moves and starting over and figuring out where God wanted us to be, just going along as things came. No real strategy or goal-setting. I've actually sworn off New Year's resolutions for a few years now. But I remember that when I did set goals, I usually hit them. I wanted to write three books under my name by the time I was thirty. I did it. I sometimes miss the drive that, during the Proverbs 31 experiment, I tried hard to set aside.

I asked Cliff what he thought about the tools I wanted to get, because maybe that's being submissive too, asking your husband before you spend anything. And of course, my sweet type B husband was cautious, and he told me I should take a look first and think about it. And I didn't like his answer.

"OK, you know what? I'll buy it if I want to." I shot Cliff a look and walked out of the room. Does it really make sense to ask his opinion when he doesn't work in my field, when he isn't a writer or doesn't design websites?

But God started tapping me on the shoulder as soon as I said it. I thought about the conversation I'd just had with Caleb about waiting for things. Could I follow my own advice? And if I'm going to ask my husband what he thinks, shouldn't I actually listen to what he says? Or at least consider it? Should I really be so quick to write it off? Besides, isn't it a good thing to have a sounding board like my husband to help me think about decisions before I make them, rather than me just plowing ahead and maybe missing something?

I thought about all of that, and then went back to Cliff and told him I was sorry.

Mutual Helping?

August has arrived. School is just about to start back, and I'm slowly getting used to the idea that our son will be a middle schooler. I'm grateful Cliff's travel has come to an end and he'll be home more often now.

It's funny, though, that just as I've been really trying to pursue what it means to be a submissive wife, an online reviewer accused me of being a feminist because of what I wrote about in my previous book. To her, asking Cliff to help me with the laundry was the equivalent of spousal heresy.

I disagree. And maybe this is where a lot of us disagree. Where the rubber meets the road. Or more accurately, where the toilet brush hits the toilet. Whose toilet brush is it?

Does the wife do it all? Does the husband? Does whoever is at home at the time? Does the husband help? Does the wife refuse the help? Does the wife insist on the help?

Why is it that husbands always describe their actions around the household as "helping"? Why don't wives do that? "I helped this morning by cleaning out the refrigerator." Doesn't it just sound better when you say, "I cleaned out the refrigerator this morning"? But husbands always seem to like this word *help*. Cliff will tell me, "Hey, I helped last night with the dishes." Why not just say, "I did the dishes"?

How have women gotten the corner of the market on housecleaning?

And why did I just ask that? We know why. Because the women before us, aka our husbands' mothers, did the cleaning for their husbands.

I'm realizing something, though. It's one thing to keep a spotless house if I'm not doing anything else. It's another thing entirely to keep a spotless house, plan great meals, and juggle the events and the projects and everything else I do.

Nowhere in the Bible do I see specific instructions that men aren't allowed to pull out a vacuum cleaner every once in a while.

As this year has progressed, I realize I've wanted our responsibilities to be spelled out that way, just a little bit. Only because it seems easier. More defined, like saying the guy gets the outside chores, the girl gets the inside chores.

But outside chores don't happen as often as inside chores. You don't mow the yard every single day (or most men don't; yours may be an exception). You do have to eat every day. So there goes that rule.

I am struggling to do it all. To pay attention to my home and my husband and my child and to spend enough time in my ministry and planning out my talks and working on my writing projects.

So I decided to sit down and talk to Cliff about it, after our family devotional on Sunday night. Our topic, interestingly enough, had been about family members helping each other.

"I'm drowning here," I told him. "I just can't do everything on my own. And I feel so stupid, because there's only three of us. It's not like I have twelve loads of laundry to do, I have three. It's not like there's a crowd of people around here to make a mess of things, there are only three of us. But I need time to focus on my work, and I also need time to focus on our family. So what am I supposed to do?"

Cliff shook his head. "Sara, you don't have to do all of this by yourself. We're a team, we help each other. You help me, I help you. Your problem is that when you're supposed to be working during the day in your office, you walk through the house and stop to do every other thing that needs to be done. You walk through the bathroom, you see a countertop that needs to be cleared. You walk through the bedroom, you see clothes that need to be picked up. You walk past the laundry room, you stop to start or fold laundry."

Wow, maybe he was paying attention.

"You just need to focus on work during the day, and I'll help when I get home at night. Leave the laundry for me. I got it."

Feeling a little more encouraged, I decided Cliff was right. I could leave some things during the day, and he could help at night.

So on Monday morning, before I sat down in my office, I pulled out the clothes in the dryer and set them on top. It was killing me not to stop right then and there and hang them up or fold them, but I thought, *No, Cliff wanted to help. I will let him help.* I set them out so he wouldn't forget.

Tuesday morning, they were still there.

Wednesday morning, they were still there. Good thing I hadn't started the next washer load or we'd have mold growing out of our towels. But still, I kept my mouth shut and stayed focused on my work. Just like my husband told me to.

When Cliff walked in the door Thursday afternoon, I was in the kitchen, getting dinner ready. After he'd had a chance to relax for a minute and say hi to Caleb, who was doing something in his room, Cliff walked back out to the kitchen.

That's when I decided to speak up.

"So, babe, when were we going to start this whole helping out thing?" I looked at him with a little smile on my face. "Laundry? Remember? You said you'd help?"

Cliff immediately looked defensive.

"I'm sorry, but I was busy last night. I was working on the floor for your new office, remember?"

I did. One of our plans when we bought the house was to convert the outside storage building into an office for me so we'd have a spare guest bedroom. My brother and his wife were coming for a visit in ten short days, and we were working hard to get the office done so we could get the guest room done. The floor was the biggest challenge. The original owners had used the space as a one-chair hair salon. The upside to that was the space had running water, electricity, and a heater/AC unit. The downside was that the linoleum floor was horrible. Stains all over it and parts of it were coming up from water damage. But scraping up the linoleum and the glue underneath had turned into a bigger chore than we'd expected.

"I understand, but you didn't help Monday or Tuesday either. I'm not mad, but I'm just pointing out that you said you would help, and so I believed you and left the laundry alone. And now none of us have towels and we'll all be naked tomorrow."

I think I'm proving the point I was trying to make when I talked to him the other night. He works all day and it's understandable he doesn't feel like doing laundry when he comes home. But I work too. So what to do about chores that still need to get done? Somebody has to do them.

I guess I either need to learn to do more on less sleep or figure out something else. Soon.

It's Getting Hot in Here

This morning when we woke up, the air conditioning wasn't working. I could feel it as I walked out of our room and into the hall. I glanced at the thermostat. Seventy-five degrees at seven a.m. Yes, that was definitely not a good sign. I sighed. We've known since we moved into the house that the AC has shown signs of wear, but Cliff has been reluctant or too busy to do anything about it.

And now we're about to pay the piper.

I just want to ask—am I so wrong for wanting established jobs and responsibilities? As much as I appreciate his help with the laundry when I need it (and when he does it), life goes much more smoothly now that I just assume the responsibility. No one fights anymore over why everyone is going to be forced to go to work and school naked, because I just make sure the laundry gets done. It's one of my (many) jobs. But I'm happy to do it because I know it helps our family.

I just wish Cliff felt the same way about house maintenance. Things flow better when there's a basic understanding of who does what most of the time, with of course the exception for when someone is out of town, or sick, or just being lazy and calls in their Get Out of Jail card for the day and the other spouse picks up their slack for a bit. Not that I would know anything about that last part.

It's good to have designated responsibilities because otherwise, it's easy to say "Oh, she'll do it," or "Oh, he'll do it," and then nothing ever gets done if no one actually does it. Is it too much to ask for him to take main- tenance man responsibilities if I'm usually the maid? Unfortunately, it usu- ally takes something breaking down before we call for a service check, and then I'm the one who usually calls anyway.

I'm thinking about all of this when Cliff walks into the kitchen for breakfast and I mention the problem with the air. That it's now 76 degrees in the house and we have it set at 75. I just turned it down to 74, and still nothing. As I flit back and forth between the thermostat and the kitchen for the third time in the last fifteen minutes, calling out to him my latest thermostat update, he's casually getting ready to leave for work. He pulls his leftovers out of the refrigerator to take with him under one arm and with the other he pulls me in for a kiss good-bye.

I look at him. Seriously? He's about to walk out the door and leave me here with no air? In late July in South Louisiana? Without even bothering to attempt a guess at what's wrong?

Is that very head of household? I think not.

I try to put a smile on my face and look at him as sweetly as I can.

"Um, honey? The air conditioner? Are you going to look at it?"

He looks at me. He'd almost escaped. He's not happy about it, but he puts his lunch back down on the counter and walks outside to take a look at the unit.

After walking around the house and doing some investigative leg work, he found two more breaker boxes in the shed where my office will be. The AC breaker was tripped, so he turned it back on and told me to give it a few hours to see if it comes back on. Another quick kiss and he's outta there.

By noon, it was 80 degrees in the house. Definitely time to call an AC guy. I check with him by text to make sure he's OK with it, and then make the call. Two hours and just thirty dollars later, the problem had been determined, and it was a very quick fix. The other breaker needed to be turned on.

Mr. Jesse, our AC technician who was repairing AC units in this town when I was a kid, sat for a minute at our kitchen counter drinking the glass of water I'd offered him after he'd spent several minutes up in our hot attic. He glanced over at our refrigerator.

"Now that is organization," he said, smiling. He pointed to the little board I had on the fridge titled "What's for Dinner?"

"Oh, that?" I asked, smiling, a little surprised he noticed. "No, that's just me trying to ensure my family doesn't starve."

"Nah, you need to give yourself a little more credit. We barely have any idea what we're gonna eat tonight, let alone four nights from tonight."

"Well, it's just easier when I have a plan."

I thanked Mr. Jesse as he left for his next job and thought about what he said. Maybe I did need to give myself a little more credit. As my husband's helper, I help keep the house functioning. I'm not supposed to do it completely by myself, but what I offer does have reward. It does have value.

I also learned something about my husband today. That just as we're not always thinking about living up to our role as helpmate, they're not always thinking about their role as head of household. It's our job to help them remember, whether they want to be reminded or not. Then thank them anyway.

The Lizard

Living in South Louisiana, we are "blessed" with an abundant population of Mediterranean geckos, these creepy-looking pink, almost translucent little lizards. At night, you can usually see them everywhere. Their eyeballs pop out of their sockets, and they look just like little pink aliens or naked deformed baby rats (with oddly shaped pointed heads). They like to assemble in mass in the ceiling frame of our carport like an ancient tribe rallying around a campfire before they strike. They're worse in the summer but hardly around during the winter, at least when it gets below 50 degrees.

These things creep me out. Probably because the first time I ever had contact with one, it was nine o'clock at night, and I'd walked outside to pull the trash cans out or something, and this thing just plopped off the top of the carport onto the concrete below, two inches from my head. For a brief second, I thought I would be one of those unfortunate people to suffer "death by lizard"—not from of the lizard's size, mind you, but from the heart attack in the wake of such surprise and lizard creepiness.

I'll never forget seeing and hearing the plop of this amphibious night creature. As I sprang back, I looked up and noticed seven more, all hanging out up in the corners of the carport. Screeching violins started playing, and I'm pretty sure my scrunched-up horrified face could have competed with Janet Leigh's in the shower scene in *Psycho*.

I marched right back into the house (OK, maybe I ran and maybe there was squealing involved) and demanded from all knowing Google the best way to kill these horrible blights on my nighttime tiptoes outside.

Unfortunately, what I read was that these little geckos are "harmless" and actually do "a wonderful thing for the environment and for house owners by eating a lot of insects, so if you have a gecko or two around, consider yourself blessed and above all, don't try to kill them."

Oh goody. Lucky me. However, later, I did meet a fellow gecko hater at a garage sale, a woman with silver hair and big earrings who told me in no uncertain terms she hairsprays the suckers into heaven, though it might feel a little like the opposite destination for the geckos because the hairspray apparently is like acid to their skin and burns them into oblivion. Old Lady doesn't care if they're good for the environment; they're not taking up residence in hers.

I thought about being like Old Lady for a brief second…but then I also thought about how much I hate spiders. And I caved. And put the hairspray canister back on my bathroom counter.

So since discovering these disgusting creatures, if I have to leave the house at all at night, I do my best to keep my head down as I run out and run in. Cliff and Caleb have gotten used to me serenading our ten-second walks from the back door to the car with "lizard, lizard, lizard" as I jump into the passenger seat and slam the door. They also chuckle about it and roll their eyes.

I don't care. I'd managed to go all summer with this system working just fine. Except for the night one was hanging out on our back door, which opens to our patio and backyard, and I didn't know it.

Until I opened the door.

Suddenly, I was two inches from the face of Gecko himself. Every centimeter of his three-inch body was mere seconds away from doing who knows what life-threatening activity.

"CLLLLLIIIIIIIFFFFF!"

"CLLIIIIIFFFFFFFFF!!!"

By the time Cliff came running and threw himself into the hall doorway, ready to body slam the serial killer who must have somehow found his way into our house and was threatening his poor precious wife, I had backed up to the wall on the other side of the room, perfecting my best imitation of Edvard Munch's painting, *The Scream*.

"*What?* Are you OK?" he asked, running to me, checking me over for blood, for gaping wounds, for broken bones, for the death that my screaming had indicated was somehow imminent.

My hand shook as I pointed toward the door eight feet away. All I could move my mouth to say was, "Li…zard…There's a *lizard*!"

Cliff took a step back and looked at me. Then he looked at the lizard. And then he looked back at me. He cocked his head and tried to hold the grin that was already spreading from one corner of his face to the other.

"I thought you were, like, dying," he said. "I thought I was getting ready to call 911."

He paused and composed himself. No doubt getting clear instructions from God on how to deal with his nutcase of a spouse who still looked as if she were posing as an extra in *Body Snatchers*.

"OK, Sara, I see the lizard," he said. "Sit down here and I'll take care of it."

He pulled out the piano bench I was standing next to, and I slowly lowered myself down to watch.

As Cliff stepped toward the door and looked closer at the lizard, which had slipped over the top of the door when I opened it and was now hanging on the inside, I held my breath and ran some stats in my head.

Cliff has about a fifty-fifty record when it comes to grabbing other kinds of unwanted things off walls. They either find their way successfully into the paper towel held in his hand, or they get dropped or knocked to the floor, scurrying around for one more shot at freedom. He has about a thirty-seventy rate of success with spiders (he isn't any more of a spider fan than I am). I had no idea how he would do with a lizard.

But he was head of our household. He was master of our domain. And all the other clichés we think of when we infer the man is in charge. And at that moment, I trusted him to do the right thing, to take care of this wretched blight that threatened our beautiful home. I was counting on him to…pull out his phone?

Yes, there my husband stood, with the door opened partway, with the lizard hanging onto the corner of the door, and Cliff stepping closer to get a good shot on his camera phone for all his Facebook buddies to see.

About the time he clicked the picture is about the time the lizard chose his moment to make a break for it.

No, not back outside where he should have gone, but a quick leap from the door to the molding directly above, up the wall and over, and then straight down the wall and under the windows, the bottoms of which were almost completely hidden from view behind our couch. And my husband's phone was still in his hand.

Cliff turned and looked over his shoulder at me. Probably no doubt making sure I wasn't going to faint. Or kill him.

Oh. My. Word. The lizard was loose. And in my house.

My mouth flew open about the same time my feet and knees pulled up.

"Cliff!" I stood up and darted to the far back corner of our living room, trying to see if I could see the lizard.

Cliff quickly (and a little sheepishly) put away his phone and hustled over to the middle of the room, peering over the couch, peeking around the edge of it.

Nothing.

"Cliff…" I began to say, with all the calm I could muster, trying to think of words in my head like *respect* and *honor* and *LIZARD* and *love* and *LIZARD*. OK, it wasn't working so well.

"Cliff, there is a lizard in my house. There is a *lizard* in my house. Please find it. Because I will not be sleeping a wink until you do."

That's right, I said my house. Not our house, not your house, my house. Because when there's a lizard in the house I call home and sanctuary, I am claiming ownership, and I want the offending party *gone*.

One hour later, I surveyed the scene. Both couches were in the middle of the room, one turned at an angle to the other, which was also at an odd angle. All the cushions were littered around them on the floor. A big flashlight sat on the floor next to Cliff. He was tired and annoyed at his big baby of a wife freaking out about a lizard only slightly bigger than a credit card, and he just wanted to go to bed.

We never found the lizard.

Somehow I did find a way to sleep that night, eventually, despite thoughts that lasted for days and weeks of some gecko with an Australian accent showing up at three a.m., sitting on top of my head and looking at me, telling me all he really wanted to know was if I had car insurance.

I'd like to think that somehow, the offending lizard found its way outside twenty minutes after it came in. Which still isn't completely comforting. Because if he could find his way out, who knows what else might be able to find its way in.

I still think about that gecko sometimes. But we've never had any more problems with geckos hanging out outside, at least not on the door.

Think his friends got the message?

The Question

I have hit a dilemma of sorts about this experiment. Other than my issues with time management, being submissive toward my husband is feeling too easy. So I don't know if that means I've entered into my stride, that helping my husband, respecting my husband, all that's involved with submitting to my husband, is now feeling second nature—or I'm somehow missing it completely. Or maybe there just haven't been any conflicts to seriously test my submission quotient in the last month.

Life is good, though nothing out of the ordinary of our usual craziness. Yesterday, I came home from running a quick errand with Caleb for his first day of school and discovered the pantry door had been left open and Sammy, our schnauzer, had managed to pull out a potato from the potato sack and eat at least two-thirds of it. He probably would have eaten all of it if we hadn't interrupted him.

I quickly got on the phone to the vet. They assured me potato wasn't bad for dogs, though there was always a chance for some stomach unpleasantness, especially since he'd eaten that much of it.

That unpleasantness came gurgling up at three the next morning when I woke up to the sounds of Sammy heaving in the corner of our dark room.

"No, no, no, no!" I begged as I hurled myself out of bed and shooed him outside toward the patio and the backyard. I heard Cliff sigh loudly from his side of the bed, barely awake. I warned him to watch his eyes as I turned on my bedside lamp.

A quick spot check revealed we'd escaped disaster. No carpet scrubbing in the middle of the night this time. I was relieved.

But morning came quickly. Today was back to school for Caleb and a pretty big deal since it's sixth grade.

Middle school. I am the mother of a middle schooler.

Sending your child to middle school is a major test for a type A mom, especially when you have a type B son. Type B sons don't pay a whole lot of attention to schedules, classes, or lists. They usually depend on their type A mothers to do it for them.

We had an intervention the other day when I sat down with Caleb and helped him get his binder organized and we reviewed the (multiple) copies of his schedule I printed out for him. I also made copies of the map the school supplied, and we traced his route from class to class and went over all of the rules and school policies. The middle school he's going to has a reputation (thanks to the strict and high standards of the principal) for being the toughest and most disciplined in the school district. At the open house about a month ago, they laid out the ground rules for what was expected and what was needed every day.

Binder, Badge (ID card), and Belt for the boys. Books came in two sets—one in the respective classrooms, one copy at home. The binder is all they carry with them. It holds all their folders, notebook paper, and pens and pencils. Backpacks aren't allowed. And the belt is just the customary part of the uniform dress code. The badge has to be worn every single day, and it's a dollar fine for every day they don't have it on.

I made sure everything Caleb needed was nicely laid out in his room or on the kitchen table and that his badge hung on the rack by the door.

So with the back-to-school schedule upon us, five a.m. came early, especially after Sammy's three a.m. wake-up call. I jumped into the shower, eager to get started back to a somewhat regular schedule, even if I was feeling a little tired.

And that's when it hit me.

Literally—the showerhead came off and almost knocked me down. Water suddenly sprayed everywhere. I managed to step back and finish getting the soap out of my hair with the stream of water that was now coming out like the end of a fire hydrant.

This morning was shaping up to be a doozy. But this was a special day, Caleb's first day of middle school, and I was determined to make the best of it.

He was already up and dressed by the time I made my way into the kitchen and fixed him a special breakfast of eggs and pancakes to get his day started right. I reviewed his schedule with him for the eighteenth time and tried giving him a pep talk.

"Ask questions if you have them," I told him. "If you get lost, just ask a teacher how to get to your class. Don't be late because you don't ask. And don't be nervous."

Caleb looked at me as he walked to the sink to put his plate up. "Um, Mom, I was fine until you just said that. Now I'm nervous."

I smiled and gave him a squeeze around his shoulders. "OK, grab your stuff and let's go. It's time!"

We said a quick prayer with Cliff, who hadn't left for work yet, and then we jumped in the car and headed off to the school. Traffic was pretty heavy as we got closer, but I'd made a point to leave early, so I knew he'd make it on time.

I gave him my usual quick, morning-mom blessing—"Listen to your teacher, be kind to your friends, do your very best, and remember God loves you and has a great big plan for you"—and bumped his fist with mine. I couldn't believe we'd done this every single morning since kindergarten. I silently wondered how long he'd still want to do it.

He gave me a quick peck on the lips and a cheery "'Bye, Mom! See you this afternoon!" and jumped out of the car. I watched with pride as he stepped into the flow of kids all walking to their classes with their binders in hand and their IDs hanging around their necks…

Oh. Crud.

Caleb's neck was sans ID, and there he was, oblivious, already too far for me to catch him.

The car line moved forward, and I had to move with it. I tried calling Cliff. No answer.

This was just great. I had visions of Caleb being pulled out of class and sent to the principal's office not just the first day of school but the first hour.

I drove as fast as the 35 miles-per-hour speed limit between the school and our house would let me, and then jumped out of the car and hurried through the back door. Sure enough, Caleb's ID was sitting right where it had been for the last month or so. Hanging by the door. Both of us had walked by without noticing.

Grabbing it, I hollered to Cliff, who was packing his lunch. "Caleb forgot his ID, gotta get it to him, he has no idea, well, by now he probably does, anyway, gotta go!"

I got back into the car and drove back to the school. There was a problem, though. The school wasn't letting parents drive into the parking lot to go into the office, which meant I had to drive back into the car line. I wasn't sure how this would work. As I pulled in, there were no other cars in front of me, and teachers were leaving their duty posts and walking toward the buildings.

I flagged down one teacher I didn't know and rolled down my window, but as I started to speak, another teacher approached. Renee was a member at our church. I breathed a sigh of relief, seeing a familiar face.

"Hey! Caleb forgot his ID!" I blurted out, holding it up with an expression of "help?" written all over my face.

Renee smiled and took it from me. "Oh, I bet he's missing this," she said, chuckling. After I told her he was in the gym for his first class, she promised to get it to him.

As I drove away and turned onto the main road, I sighed big. Well, it wasn't the best first day back to school, but at least it wouldn't be starting in the principal's office.

When I picked Caleb up that afternoon, he got into the car and sighed a big sigh.

"How did it go?" I asked.

He leaned back into his seat, his eyes forward.

"I am a changed man," he said.

That night at dinner, we enjoyed listening to Caleb talk about his day (and his near miss of getting into trouble because he'd forgotten his ID). Afterward, as Cliff and I were rinsing off the dishes and loading them into the dishwasher, I asked him the question I'd wanted to ask for a few days.

After I explained that things were feeling too easy, and I was concerned I wasn't doing enough to be submissive (seriously—is what I just wrote not complete irony?), I said, "What is something you wish I'd do, and what's something you wish I wouldn't do?"

Cliff put the last plate in the dishwasher and looked at me. "Other than ask these questions?"

I just looked at him.

He leaned back against the counter and thought for a moment. "I think one thing you've already done is that you're letting me find my own way as the leader for our home and not trying to push me into whatever you think a leader should be."

"Really? How so?"

"Well, like the other night when we were supposed to do our family devotion. You asked me once about it and then you left it at that. You didn't nag, you didn't harp about it, you left it up to me whether we were going to get to it that night or not. I liked that."

I'd had no idea he noticed. That moment had been hard for me, too, because I'd wanted to "help" him by reminding him of the importance of doing it consistently. But I'd remembered something Beth Moore has said about the fact that we cannot be our husband's Holy Spirit, and I figured if we can't be his Holy Spirit for his personal relationship with Christ, we can't really be his Holy Spirit as head of household for his family, either. So I sat in the living room and read a book on my iPad and waited. And eventually, he walked out of the game room and said, "OK, time for our family devotion."

"OK, so what's something you wish I *didn't* do?" I asked, really curious about what he'd say.

"I already said—not to ask these questions." Cliff smiled and kissed me on the cheek before he turned back around to what he was doing.

He was right. I probably analyze things way too much. Think about things more than I need to. It seemed lately God was trying to teach me that I really need to just let go of some things while I hold tight to others. But discerning what to let go of and what to hold on to is the million dollar question.

When the Right Words Come Through Our Husbands

The more I focus on my marriage and my family, the harder it seems to focus on the other things in my life. Writing, ministry, speaking. They're all things I love to do. I feel a call from God to do these things, but I still struggle.

I get overwhelmed.

I lose confidence and grow doubt.

The boat starts to get knocked around, and I stop looking to Jesus for my answers and more to the scary storm that's surrounding me. My fears. My insecurities.

And that's how Cliff found me one night, sitting on the edge of our bed, going over the same questions that have nagged and pulled at me since I started the Proverbs 31 experiment. And now, when you throw in this whole idea of submission, this act of helping, of offering and not taking, giving and not expecting…it can be breathtaking. And not in a good way.

I'm trying to do it all and feeling like none of it is being done well. Part of me longs to just pick one thing. Just do one thing. Be a housewife and a mom. Or focus on ministry and not stress or worry or be concerned over housework. (OK, that's just fantasy, because there will always be housework.) Maybe it's not realistic or possible to do it all, at least all at once.

I told Cliff about the dream I'd had the night before. I was being squeezed to death by an enormous snake. It was terrifying, and I woke up with the question, am I doing what I'm supposed to be doing?

Cliff patiently listened while the tears rolled down and the frustration gurgled up. He took my hands in his and looked straight into my eyes.

149

"You are your hardest critic. But Caleb and I are good. Our family is great. Nothing in life is perfect, but you make me happy. We're happy together, right?"

I nodded, wiping a tear away.

"Maybe this will sound too much like a Sunday school kind of answer, but Sara, what if it's the devil who's trying to make you doubt? If he can just convince you, if he can just make you struggle just enough, throw just one more obstacle in your way, one more setback, one more discouragement, you'll quit. You'll give up. You'll take your ball and go home. You'll finally agree that the pressure is too much and you can't do it anymore. But here's the question I want you to think about. What if there's more God has for you to do?"

I sat there, thinking about Cliff's question and silently thanking God for using my husband to focus me back to him. It was the first time I could remember Cliff leading me spiritually. And I so needed it and wanted it. There was a sense of relief I could feel starting to spread in my heart and my spirit. And though I knew I had a long way to go in learning how to focus on everything that mattered, there was something so truthful to his words.

What if there *is* more God has for me to do? Was I going to let fear and doubt win? Was I going to let the enemy win?

I couldn't. And once again, even as I tried so hard to be his helper, to be his encourager, Cliff had helped and encouraged me. And even more than that, he had led.

When Kindness Is Returned

This week is a busy week for us as we work to get the office done before my brother and his wife come to visit and I head out of town for another speaking gig.

I've started noticing major differences in Cliff. He's gotten a lot more involved at church, helping weekly with the kids ministry. He runs sound and video while I lead worship. It's a family affair and we enjoy it, even if it means missing out on a full Sunday school class of our own since we usually have to cut out a little early so we can be ready when the kids get out of their classes.

He's become more vocal about his faith—he's talking more with me about God, sharing more and not just waiting for me to ask him questions. Maybe he's just figured out that if he talks first, he can choose the topic. But he's also getting up earlier on Sunday mornings and catching the live stream of our old church in South Carolina as we get ready for our church service here in Louisiana. He talks to me about the sermons and Scripture that's applicable. The other day, he even texted me from work to let me know he was praying for me as I got ready for my weekend to speak. That was huge.

It's occurring to me as I have stepped back from trying to run everything, or at least thinking that I need to run everything, that Cliff has had space to actually step forward and lead. It's kind of like a marathon runner who would really like to just open up and run at his own pace instead of lingering behind the person in front of him who is weaving all over the track and refusing to let anyone pass.

Which makes me wonder: Have I weaved all over the track in the years before this, determined to hold the lead, insisting that I be in front?

In all likelihood, yes.

I am learning that even with my determined spirit or focused personality, I don't have to be that way with my husband. I can be kind, I can be caring, I can seek his advice and his opinion without feeling as though it may undermine or devalue my own. And I can definitely do that when I see the value God has placed on Cliff's role as my husband. The gifting he is to me. The blessing he is to me.

Sometimes that blessing may seem like a diamond in the rough. It's harder to notice at times.

When I came back from my trip this weekend, I was still thinking about how our relationship is changing. My plane arrived after nine p.m., and I was excited to see Cliff and Caleb waiting for me in the pickup lane when I walked out of the airport. I'm trying to get better at switching from speaker or ministry leader and back to caring wife and mom, no matter how tired I am. I smiled big as I got into the car and reached back for Caleb's hand and leaned over to kiss Cliff.

"Hi guys, did you miss me?" I exclaimed as I settled into the seat and we headed toward home. As much as I enjoy getting to hang out with military wives, I love coming home and being with my guys. I talked a little bit about how the trip had gone, what a great group it had been, and some of the different things I got to see.

My contact had dried out as I'd dozed on the plane, so I pulled down the sun visor to take a quick look in the mirror.

And a tiny baby lizard dropped onto my hand in my lap.

"Ahhhh! Lizard!"

I flung that nasty, rubbery little shrimp onto the floorboard and immediately my legs came up.

Cliff and Caleb were laughing. They had no idea where it had come from.

"How did that thing get in the car?" I said through my squealing, half laughing, half crying at the ridiculousness of it all.

It was pitch black in the car except when we drove by the occasional streetlight. There was no way I was putting my feet down until I could open the door and run.

After fifteen unbearably long minutes, we made it to the house, and I ran in. We half-suspected the lizard had fallen into my large open purse, so Cliff told me to put it on top of the car and he would go through it.

As I walked through the door, glad to be done with the whole lizard craziness and ready to roll up my sleeves and start cleaning after being away for two days, I stopped mid-kitchen.

Everything was clean. Nothing was out on the counters. The sink was wiped down. There was no food or gunk on the stove. There was nothing on the kitchen table or clutter on the floor in the game room.

My guys had cleaned. They'd vacuumed and picked up and even wiped down the bathrooms. The last load of laundry was rolling around in the dryer. There was nothing for me to do but rest.

I woke up the next morning at four thirty and spent some alone time with God, and then went for a run after my Bible reading. As I stood in the kitchen, drinking a glass of water, I was surprised to see Cliff walk out just before six, completely dressed and ready for work. He fed the dog while I woke up Caleb. He must have noticed my surprise because he smiled and said, "I seem to recall someone saying they'd help more. That's what I'm doing."

It was one of the nicest Mondays I'd had in a while.

Hurricane

Living just a few hours from the Gulf Coast, we don't concern ourselves with blizzards or earthquakes or tornados (much). Around here, the weather threat we get most worried about is a hurricane.

Cliff and I didn't live here when Hurricane Katrina or Gustav came through, but we still see the impact both of those storms had on our town. With Katrina, the most noticeable difference is the town grew, by a lot. Many, many families and residents from around the New Orleans area headed this way after the storm and never went back. It affected housing, it affected the schools, and it definitely affected traffic. I still get tickled when I ride in the car with Ms. Nancy and we're sitting at a traffic light. She'll invariably exclaim as she watches cars driving past her in the opposite lane, "I haven't seen one person I know yet!" That's how much of a change has occurred since the hurricanes.

These people also learned from Gustav that you don't play around with hurricanes. Gustav brought a lot more direct damage to this area and left a lot of families without power for almost a week, if not close to two in certain areas. If you didn't have a generator, you were out of luck. And even if you did have a generator, finding the gas to keep it running was a long shot.

That's where we are today. Hurricane Isaac is about to make landfall in a short twenty-four hours, and all of us around here are battening down the hatches, especially since all forecasts indicate the storm is headed straight for Baton Rouge—and us.

I'd already heard the horror stories from Heather and some of the other women in our Sunday school class about the previous hurricanes, so I tried to stay calm for this one but be prepared. I'm a planner—I like to prepare for the worst and always hope for the best. But Cliff is a little more the opposite—he expects the best and figures he'll deal with the worst if it happens. I guess my thing is I don't want to have to deal with the worst.

With our money already tight, we decided we would not buy a generator. We had no idea whether the power would go out, so we decided to focus on food and supplies. I ran down a mental list of things we had: a camping stove (which has never been used), a lantern. We'd just made a trip to Sam's and stocked up on meat and chicken, and that's what I was most nervous about. I'd hate to see all of it get ruined because the power went out.

I finalized with Cliff, who was still at work in Baton Rouge, our list of what we needed and ran to the grocery store near our house. I was confident until I started walking down the aisles. The place was packed, and things were disappearing off the shelves.

So this is what it's like in a crisis, I thought. I didn't like the feeling. People seemed a little desperate, and I watched a woman put five milk jugs and two dozen boxes of Pop-Tarts into her shopping cart, and I had to wonder, did she really need all of that?

I managed to find everything we need, mainly because it was a small list, and added one box of Pop-Tarts and one more case of bottled water. But what I didn't find was batteries for the flashlights. Those were completely gone. I stood there in the hardware section (yes, this grocery store has a hardware section) trying to figure out what to do, when a store employee came walking down the aisle holding packages of flashlights with batteries included. By the time he got to the end of the aisle, he had no more packages in his hand. But one of them was in mine.

I also grabbed three Sterno fuel cans for our camping stove after calling Cliff to make sure I had the right ones. I told him how crazy it was in the store, and I asked again, trying to keep calm, "Are you sure you don't want me to get anything else? Are you sure we don't need to stock up on extras?"

My question hung out there for a while. As the leader for our home, I wanted to trust Cliff to protect us. I wanted to rely on him to provide. But this is the man who often forgets to lock the doors at night before getting into bed, and so a tiny little part of me worried that when it counts the most, he'll be too trusting or too laid-back, and he won't be the only one dealing with his decision not to do anything.

Cliff tried to reassure me. "We're good, Sara, we don't need any extra food."

"OK, we don't need any extra food," I repeated back slowly, emphasizing the words. Is it wrong that I'm repeating it just so I can confidently blame it all on him if we do need extra food a week from now?

I was trusting him to make the right decision for our family and trying to respect his decisions. But it's hard when I'm feeling like the squirrel who wants to find and stash away as many nuts as possible for the scary winter, and he's more like the lion who figures he'll just go out and kill it if we need something.

But I knew I could still help while relying on him to be the decision maker. After I got back home, I made sure all our flashlights were stocked with batteries, though we didn't really have any spares. I pulled out candles and tealights and lighters just in case. And after clearing it with Cliff first, I called my mom and insisted she come over and stay with us in the guestroom. Mom always chuckles at my overpreparedness, but she didn't argue with me. I made sure the guest room was nice and clean and all ready for her when she did come over.

The next thing on my list was to get a pile of sandbags. I picked up Caleb at the close of the school day and drove over to the field where the city had set up a sandbag station. I breathed a sigh of relief when I realized there was an entire high-school baseball team out there performing their community service by filling up sandbags and loading them into people's cars. I asked for ten, and they quickly loaded them up for us.

Cliff was touched after I called him on our way home and told him about the help we got. Later, after he came home and we decided to grab a bite to eat at the little Mexican place near where we picked up the sandbags, he asked me to drop him off. He wanted to help some other people fill up their bags.

I did what he asked, and then after Caleb and I ate, we stopped by the field to pick up Cliff. As I sat in my car, watching him load up someone else's bags, I thought about this whole idea of leading and following. It is easy to follow someone who leads like this—with compassion and integrity and true interest in helping others. I thought about what a great example he is for our son, and I know where Caleb gets his earnestness to help other people.

When Cliff got in the car, a little dirty, a little grimy but smiling (and hungry), I asked him how it went.

"Oh, it went great," he said as he rubbed his hands together to take off some of the dust. "I got a lot of weird looks, especially from the folks we know from church who drove up to get their bags. They would ask, 'Cliff, are you here to get your bags?' and I'd say, 'Oh, I already got mine. I just wanted to help some other folks too.' One guy I told that to, I noticed he put his bags in his car and then walked over to another pile and started helping load those up. So all in all, pretty good."

I told him how proud I was, and as usual, he brushed it off. But I knew he felt good too.

After we got home, it was time to settle in. The rain was supposed to start that night, heavy and fierce, and Mom planned on coming over after she stopped at her place to pack a suitcase and pick up some things.

Before he left Baton Rouge, Cliff had stopped at an electronics store and picked up one of the last weather radios they had in stock. As he showed it to me, I was impressed. It could run off a battery or electricity, and a windup handle let you crank it manually to store up power. It could also run on solar energy. You could plug your phone in and your iPad. The fact that he found this for us comforted me.

The Horns texted and invited everyone over for dinner. They were grilling before the storm came in. We sat down and talked about the forecast and how crazy it had been in the store earlier. As I rattled off my list of everything I'd done to get ready, Ms. Nancy's eyes got big and she started laughing.

"All I did was buy an extra case of water," she said, smiling big and making me feel the size of an ant. An ant that likes to store things for hurricanes. "I'm thinking it's not going to be that bad."

I took a breath. She was probably right. The hundreds of people I'd just left at the grocery store were probably all silly too.

We managed to keep our power until the next evening, right after we'd finished dinner. Cliff was home since his job had canceled work for the next two days. Though it had stormed all day, and the power flickered off and on a couple of times, I'd tempted fate by making homemade pizza for lunch. Mom, on the other hand, had to go in to work, but she was only ten minutes from the house and they expected to leave a little early. We lost cable and Internet halfway through the day, and we were all sitting at the table playing a board game when the lights finally went out.

I jumped up and grabbed the flashlight I'd placed on the desk in the kitchen and made my way to the hall closet where I kept a box of canning jars. I'd bought them about three months earlier because I'd hoped to can some green beans with Mom and Heather, but at the last minute, Heather chickened out—something about a bad experience with a canning seal once—and Mom and I just never did get together to do it. So now the canning jars would become tealight holders.

Quickly, I pulled out the glasses and added tealights to each one. Cliff and Caleb and Mom helped me set them around. We put some on the kitchen table and some on the mantel in the living room, on top of the piano, and then a few in each bedroom. I wasn't sure how long tealights would last, but I had a few dozen so I figured we were good. And if we still needed something, we always had the new pack of candles I'd bought that day from the store, though they were scented vanilla, and I'm pretty sure Cliff wasn't that excited about them.

We sat around the table and continued our game. There is something about sitting in candlelight that brings perspective you don't always get.

Eventually, Mom and Caleb headed to bed, each with their own little tealight candle in a jar as well as a flashlight. I made sure Caleb's candle was out by the time he went to sleep. Cliff and I listened to the radio and checked our phones, since we still had battery power and were still getting a signal, even if we couldn't use our Wi-Fi signal.

The next morning, Caleb was still sleeping when Cliff and I woke up. Power was still out. And the temperature was already feeling warm in the house. Our friend LaShae texted to ask if I wanted to come down and charge my phone. They'd bought a tiny generator for the last hurricane and had set it up outside with an extension cord running into the living room, where they'd slept last night, charging a fan and a power strip. I walked down to her house, and we sat on the porch and drank coffee for about an hour.

Because of power outages, the schools stayed closed the rest of the week. Our power came back on at noon, and I was grateful. The thermostat read just a little over 82 degrees. It would have gotten pretty miserable, pretty fast had the power not come back on.

Removing the Governor

We survived the hurricane and life returned to normal. Caleb went back to school, Cliff went back to work, and I came back to…everything else. I've realized something these last many months as I've walked and often limped through this journey.

There is some unfinished business left. There is a shadow creeping around the light I discovered when I went through the Proverbs 31 experiment, and I think it is threatening this experiment that I'm walking through now.

I've been living with fear. I've been sleeping with it. I've held on to it the way a small child holds on to their security blanket. Except this is no security for me. Well, maybe it is.

I realize that as I have struggled with balancing work—whether it's my writing or speaking, whether it's things with my ministry or even substitute teaching—I realize there's a fear there.

I am one Afraid Woman Walking, and I'm fearful of one very major thing: that I will go back to the way that I was—the woman so intent on her own pursuits that she's oblivious to her family's; the wife with such passion for her activities that it surpasses the passion she has for her husband; the mom so focused on being the perfect supermom (or maybe just a better version of mom than she feels she really is) that she ends up spending more time trying to be a great mom than just being one.

When I think about how much I've changed in the last two years, I'm grateful to God for how he's worked in my life. Back then, I hated doing laundry. And now I just do it and really don't mind it. Back then, I dreaded cooking dinner and putting away dishes and doing all those boring, mundane activities we call chores that are necessary to live. And now I've just embraced those things. I love keeping a clean house for my family, I love planning delicious meals and yummy desserts and making special things to share, like with our small group when it's our turn for breakfast on Sunday mornings.

But God's also called me to other things, and I think that's what I mean by fear being a security blanket of sorts. I am safe, surrounded by the people I love and the things I do in my home. Part of that is a nurturing that comes from what I do as a helper, as the thermostat I call myself. I set the temperature for my family, and over the last couple of years, that temperature has felt much better.

To step out and invest in other things besides my family and my home requires a lot more risk. I struggle to know if that risk is worth it. I don't want to go back to the way it was, when I lived for the risk and neglected what I already had.

So I sit in a holding pattern with my gears stuck in neutral, not wanting to rush forward too fast, and so I don't move at all. And Cliff finally said something to me about it. He asked me why I haven't spent more time in my office, the room we worked so hard to create, the space I've always wanted, because now it seems I want nothing to do with it.

We sat on our bed, as we often do with these heart-to-hearts that I love and he's grown to love, and through sobs and tears running down my face, I let out the fear that I've held in for so long. I was just honest. I just said it.

"I don't want to go back," I said. "I don't want to be the high-on-ambition-and-accomplishment person I left back where we were before we came here. I realize, though, that I'm holding us back. That my resistance to work because of my fear of morphing back into this person I don't want to be is keeping our family from moving forward. I know we can use the extra income. I know God has called me to ministry and to writing. I know you support me in what I do. But I don't want to go back to the way it was. I don't want to go back to the way I was."

Cliff looked at me and cupped his hands tighter around mine and pulled me close to his chest. I could feel it rising and falling as we sat there for a minute in silence. Every few seconds I sniffed and wiped away an escaping tear.

We've done this a lot. When one of us is upset, or we argue or get into a huge fight, one of us (usually Cliff) calls for our Hug. One of the first years we were married, we started doing this. For twenty seconds, we put our arms around each other and we don't let go. We may be mad when we start, but usually by the end, we've softened, we've melted, we've come together again. Cliff's hug reminds me we're in this together.

"Have I ever told you about what a governor does?" Cliff asked me.

It seemed like a strange request at this moment. And I didn't know Cliff really cared about politics. Or why he felt the need to bring it up right now.

"A governor is a device that's put in a car to prevent that car from going faster than a certain speed," Cliff said. "Trucking companies do it sometimes to make sure their drivers don't speed. Some car companies do it at the factory to make sure the car isn't driven faster than the tires can handle. It's designed to be a limiter—it limits the car from going as fast as it could."

He looked hard into my eyes. "I think you've done that to yourself. I think you've given yourself a governor, and I'm telling you, Sara, you can take it out. We're not the same people we were when we first got married. You're not the same, I'm not the same. We've grown, we've changed, and I think a whole lot for the better. God worked in our lives then, and he's working in our lives now. We recognize where we don't want to be. And I'm confident you won't ever be like the woman you're so afraid of becoming again. You're better than that. I'm better than I was. We've grown and we've grown together. Now, you need to have confidence in that growth."

I thought about his words and my heart felt a little lighter. I know he's right. I know I've been holding myself back. I've been afraid to push the accelerator even just a little.

Sometimes I think how perfect it would be if God would just pass out boxes to his children, and each one of us fit in one perfectly. It was our size, our shape, and as long as we stayed inside that discrete little box, we'd know we were OK.

But it doesn't work like that, does it. God is so much bigger than the boxes we try to put ourselves in with labels we create for ourselves. He's given me the blessing of being a wife, of being a mom, and he's given me definite specifics in Scripture on what that looks like. But he's also left a lot for me to try and understand by pursuing his heart in earnest, studying his Word, and relying on his Holy Spirit to guide me. Not to make it up as I go along, but to pursue his leading on what I do, and when I do it, and how I do it. And I'm realizing that trying to establish blanket rules limits me, and it limits God. It limits God from working through me to achieve whatever means he desires, because we assume God isn't big enough to show us how he wants us, so we need to rely on what others say, or what culture dictates, or what the crowd thinks is acceptable.

I will never believe that the trips I took to the Middle East as a reporter and writer when my son was just two years old were a mistake, even though the women I worked with at the time questioned me. Repeatedly. Those trips opened doors to things that opened doors to other things. Over the years, there have been blessings and challenges and mistakes…but isn't it all worth it in the end if it brings us closer to God and his purpose for us?

I'm realizing that to understand God's desire and design for my role in my marriage, for my role in my relationship with my husband, I have to focus in on him and what Scripture says, and then be confident enough in his strength and his understanding to just keep going.

Questions are good, but when we get the answers, continuing to ask the same questions doesn't work. We're no longer being obedient; we're just being stubborn.

I have a long way to go, but I want to recognize when I get the answers God's given me. And have the confidence in his strength and in his time to keep moving.

No limits.

No weights.

No governor.

Where I'm Supposed to Be

Still feeling a little weary, I got ready for another trip and boarded a plane Friday morning for a women's conference in Birmingham. This was a new kind of event for me because so much of what I've done up till now has been dedicated solely to military wives. But since the Proverbs 31 book came out, I've started getting a few new opportunities to talk to more women about being a wife and mom.

I was glad for the opportunity, but I was mentally run down. When I arrived at the hotel, I learned that my workshops were in different rooms and at different times than what was printed in the official program guide. This made it pretty confusing for anyone who'd thought about coming, though the organizers did their best to get the word out to the ladies in attendance.

Still, I made the best of it. I was excited about this first workshop because it was specifically for military wives. Since the conference wasn't a military wives event, I was curious to see who all might come. I made a point to get to the workshop location about twenty minutes before my workshop was to start. But there was a problem. The workshop before mine was running late—as in seriously late. The leader was supposed to already have wrapped up, and she was still talking, with the door shut.

I tried not to stress about it, but she kept going, and by the time her group did start to leave the room, my workshop was supposed to have already started. I hadn't even had the chance to set up my laptop yet. As I tried to politely walk through the sea of women exiting, I noticed the workshop leader was still chatting. I took a breath, smiled, and did my best to work around her to get set up.

But nothing was going right. The projector wouldn't work for the presentation I'd planned, and by the time the tech guy came and went, having brought a second projector (which didn't cooperate either), I finally got my group started almost twenty-five minutes late. By that point, I was just silently asking God to help me through it. The eight military wives who attended were gracious and sweet and listened, but I wasn't at all sure if anything I said really resonated. Everything just felt off.

By dinner time, I was feeling pretty sorry for myself. As usual, I had come to this event by myself, and at this kind of event, a conference for moms, most attendees come with somebody. Sometimes I wish God had made me a lot less independent. Though I knew a lot of the ladies on the conference leadership team, they were all pretty busy with specific responsibilities for the weekend, so I was by myself.

The schedule for the evening was dinner on your own, and only one or two eating options were available in the hotel. As I stood in line by myself, I tried talking and getting to know the women around me. I was excited to discover the two ladies behind me were from Nashville, our old stomping grounds. We chatted about our families and how long they'd known each other, and I found out they were good friends who'd decided to meet up to come to this event. Ever hopeful, I wondered if I might be able to eat dinner with them, and just as I was starting to warm up to ask them if that would be all right, a waiter called "Table for two?" and they were out of there, without another glance in my direction. And I was again on my own, eventually getting a table for one.

I sat at my table, alone, with a hundred other women surrounding me, all talking and laughing, and tried to choke down my food so I could just get out of there. It felt more and more like God was confirming that this wasn't my gig. Maybe this wasn't even my calling. The doubts swirled, and all I wanted to do was go home.

That night in my hotel room, as I reviewed notes for my second workshop, I questioned God about the whole thing. Had I missed something? Was I really supposed to be there? Did he really need me? Why was I there in the first place?

The next morning, after spending time praying and worshiping in my hotel room, I decided to skip the general session and focus on getting ready for my afternoon workshop. My expectations were very low though for how the day was going to turn out. I felt a quiet resignation about the whole thing, but before I left my room, I spoke a quiet prayer to God.

"Jesus, you alone know why I'm here. Just let me stay focused on you."

After packing up and checking out at the front desk, I headed over to find the room where my workshop was going to be. Luckily, there was no one ahead of me this time, and so I took my time setting everything up. I'd already decided I wasn't even going to attempt to use my laptop this time and would settle for good old-fashioned speaking without the slides. After setting everything out and praying that God would encourage the women who came, I decided to get coffee and find somewhere to look over my notes once again.

By now, the general session had already started and so there were very few women out in the main area where the coffee shop was located. There was a peaceful, subdued quietness about the place as I stood in the short line made up mostly of conference staff members. No doubt people were still waking up. I noticed a woman about my age, maybe a little older, with short dirty-blond hair, step in line behind me.

I stood with my eyes looking straight ahead, but an internal conversation was already going. I felt God speaking to me, nudging me to turn around and say hello. I wanted to fight it, to remind him of the loneliness I'd felt just the night before, the attempts I'd made to reach out and the cold shoulders I'd received in return. I was tired, and I was licking wounds that weren't visible to anyone in that line.

But still, God nudged me to turn around and say hello to this woman I didn't know, this mom who probably was tired and just needed coffee to wake up and had no desire to start a conversation of any kind. It didn't matter, though, to God. He pressed into my heart the words, *keep trying.*

So I did.

I turned around, and with a smile, I said hello and asked her if she was enjoying the conference (she was) and if this was her first time (it was). I told her my name was Sara. Hers was Sandra. As we stood there chatting, one of the conference staff members came up to me.

"Sorry to interrupt, Sara, but we found a podium for your room that you wanted," she said.

"Oh, thank you, that's perfect," I told her.

"Wait a minute," Sandra said, looking at me funny. "Are you a speaker?"

"Oh, no, I'm just a workshop leader," I said.

"What's your last name?"

When I told her, her face showed shock. "I've read every one of your books! Our small group at church just finished your last one. I saw you were coming to this and I was really hoping to meet you. My friend is going to be so sorry she didn't come get coffee with me!"

It was fun to meet someone who has actually read what I've written, but what she said next was what I really cared about. Sandra's husband had just retired from the army after twenty-three years and several deployments. Gradually, as we talked more, she shared with me that he was dealing with severe post-traumatic stress disorder. For the next several minutes, as we waited to get our coffee and then after we had steaming cups in our hands, we talked, and I was able to encourage her and suggest some resources she could check out and pray with her in a little corner of the lobby.

Neither one of us could get over the God-moment we'd just experienced.

She kept telling me, "I had no idea why I needed to get up and leave the main session to go get coffee, of all things, but now I know!" She gave me a big hug before heading back to the session, eager to tell her friend.

I knew something too. Just as God had used me to encourage her, God used that sweet military wife to encourage me—and through her, he showed me exactly why I was supposed to be at that conference that weekend.

If there were no other reason for me to be there—through all the doubt, all the heart weariness I'd felt the night before—God had reminded me in a powerful way that his plan is not always my own. That if there were no other reason for me to be there, it was for that wife at that moment to have that encouragement.

I prayed silently, thanking him for that blessing and giving him the rest of my time there. And then I headed over to my workshop room to get ready. About forty minutes before it was to start, two women walked in and sat in the front row. I checked the time on my phone, a little puzzled.

"What time does the next workshop start?" I asked them, wondering if I had my time wrong.

"Oh, you've still got thirty minutes or so, but we wanted to make sure we got a seat," one of the ladies said. "We thought this one would probably fill up fast."

I didn't know where they were getting their information, but OK.

Though I hadn't counted, there looked to be about fifty or so chairs in the room. Considering I'd had eight ladies in my previous workshop, I was keeping my expectations pretty low for this one.

As the time drew closer, more and more women started coming in. Chairs were filling up, and the room was getting noisy. *Oh my word, there are people in here!* I thought to myself. Pretty soon, women were bringing chairs in, and several came and sat on the floor by my feet. Some ended up leaving because of the lack of space. One of the conference volunteers counted before the end of the session and over a hundred and twenty women were packed into that tiny little room.

We had a great session about the Proverbs 31 wife—or more specifically, how to approach the Proverbs 31 wife from a normal, stressed-out, far-from-perfect perspective. But the thing I will remember most about that weekend was Sandra, the military wife who got in line behind me for coffee.

Sometimes God has us somewhere for a very specific purpose. And sometimes he has us in place for a very specific person.

Maybe on many days as wives, that specific person is our husband. But God also uses us to bless friends or other family members or complete strangers. As I continue to study this whole idea of submission, I want to make sure I don't miss God's plan and where he wants me.

True submission really does start with him.

Is Being Kind to Our Husbands Brainwashing?

shared something on one of my Facebook pages after I got back from the conference. One of the women in my second workshop had asked a really good question. She wanted to know: "How can I not be resentful when it feels like I do everything and my husband, well, doesn't?"

This is what I wrote:

> Have you been there? You're cleaning, working, juggling— and your husband is sitting. Sitting watching TV. Sitting with the paper. Sitting in front of a video game. It can feel so incredibly frustrating. And annoying. And downright unfair.
>
> How can he not see everything that needs to be done? And worse, if he can see, how can he ignore it?
>
> Over the last couple of years, I've learned something that helps me ignore (most days) the resentment bug that so often wants to rise up in my heart.
>
> I wear kindness. When I actively attempt to be kind to my husband, doing things while he doesn't or when it seems I'm doing more than he is, it doesn't feel so unfair. Instead, it feels like I'm giving something very special. A blessing. It doesn't feel like I'm a slave. Or being slighted. Just that I'm doing kindness for my family. I'm offering a gift when the kitchen is nice and clean and I put his clothes away when I'm really tempted to just leave them in the laundry room and let him get them five days from now when he finally remembers he has that pair of pants

and goes looking for them. Yes, I have so many things I'm doing and want to do. But I know God has given me my husband and my child too.

I remember, too, that men are singular-thinking (that's how they're genetically wired) and God made me a multitasker for a reason. Because my husband needs me that way. How else would dinner, homework, and bill paying get done at the same time?

I'm learning to see what I do as not just "a mom thing" but a *heart* thing.

I set the tone for my home. I influence the temperature. I move the thermostat. My actions weigh more than I may know.

So if I'm always looking at "The List" and who does more or who does less, then I may miss seeing a blessing.

And a bonus blessing? As I've strived to be more kind, I'm seeing my husband respond the same way. He helps more. He sees more. And wow, that's nice. But it's not my reason any more for why I'm kind. It's because God's asked me to be.

So the next time you find yourself aggravated and feeling like everything is on you and no one is helping…ask who you're doing it for? And ask the One who truly cares to help you see the blessing you really are.

Ephesians 5:1-2—"Therefore, be imitators of God, as dearly loved children. And walk in love, as the Messiah also loved us and gave Himself for us, a sacrificial and fragrant offering to God."

A lot of women were thankful for a new way of looking at this age-old dilemma, but a few didn't appreciate it all that much. One woman outright hated it. She wrote: "Kindness? Really. I think not. More like misinformed brainwashing," and pointed out that the Bible was written by all men so we as women should take heed and not even try to follow it.

I've heard that argument before, and in the context of submission. Shoot, I've probably thought it myself. But saying we shouldn't heed those verses because the Bible was written by men doesn't make sense. Not if we believe the part about salvation and God's grace and what his Son did on a cross for us. Because that was written by men too.

Thinking about what the commenter said made me realize that if we really do earnestly try to follow what the Bible says—whether toward our husbands or our children, or just working to honor God in all that we do—we will probably look pretty strange to other people. We won't make much sense. We may come off odd. Or to some people, brainwashed.

But I stand by being kind to my husband. It's not easy. It's extremely difficult sometimes, and there are moments where I fail and fail again.

I think it goes back to what I've said before. Following God isn't about what God can do for us. It's about what we can do for God. How we serve him. How we love him. How we honor him with our lives.

Marriage is about two people, but it's also about two relationships. My relationship with God and my relationship with my husband. As I grow closer to God, my desire should also be to grow closer to my husband. To love him more. Treat him more kindly. Show him honor. Be intentional about helping. And be willing to be selfless.

It won't always happen. It may be a struggle. But I believe there are still blessings in the blunders.

In Ministry Together

This weekend is an important one. We are headed to Little Rock, Arkansas, for a Tour of Duty Live event, the weekend retreat I lead for military wives going through deployment. I say "we" because Cliff is coming with me, as well as a couple of guys from our church who are leading praise and worship.

I'm excited but nervous. Normally, Cliff helps me pack everything up and leave, but he doesn't get to come. Usually he has a drill weekend or some other navy or work commitment he has to do. But this time, my mom is staying with Caleb, and Cliff gets to come along. This will be the first time he gets to hear me speak. I'm so glad he gets to go.

But I'm also feeling a little challenged. Because I tend to snap at Cliff when I'm stressed, which is usually during the couple of days leading up to an event. I want to be sweet and loving and respectful to him. And even though I have a lot on my mind as I want to minister to and encourage the women who will be there at the retreat this weekend, I want to be kind and honoring and intentional toward him.

As we got things packed up and the car loaded, though, I could already feel things getting tense. We stood in the kitchen, and I grabbed his hand.

"Can we take a second and pray before we go pick up Andrew and Laremy?" I asked him.

We stood there and prayed for each other and for the retreat, for the women coming and for Andrew and Laremy. I was so excited and thankful Cliff was going to be there, and I couldn't wait to see what God would do.

From Louisiana to Arkansas, there is not a lot to see. The ground is flat and the scenery is dull. Cliff had insisted on driving, and so I sat shotgun while Andrew and Laremy had the backseat. We were riding in our new-to-us Highlander Cliff and I had just bought the weekend before. This was a new experience for me. Normally, it's just me heading to an event. Now I was on the road with three guys. It was fun until they started talking about movies. And wrestling. And music. Guys talk way different than girls do. But I was glad Cliff was enjoying some guy time.

We got to the hotel, which was right next to the church, about ninety minutes before we were scheduled to begin. Cliff insisted that I hang back in the hotel room and rest for a few minutes while he and the guys went over to the church to set up. I wasn't used to this either. I tried to rest, but I thought about what I was sharing that night. Also, one of my close friends, Shauna, was meeting us there. She serves on our Wives of Faith board and is our executive director. I was excited that she could be there to be part of the weekend too. I was grateful to God for how he'd brought everything together for this, and for the church that had seen the vision for it.

It was a small group that met Friday night and Saturday, but they were all military wives going through deployments. I like small groups because it offers more of a chance to meet each other and talk. For our first session, I shared what it means to rely on God's strength and how so often we try to rely on our own. We like to believe we can "put on our big girl panties" and just carry on, but it doesn't always work that way. Usually, it doesn't work that way.

The session went well, and the women responded afterward with good conversation and lots of connections with each other.

After everyone had cleared out, Cliff and I headed back to the hotel. It was going to be a late night for me since I still needed to look over my messages for the next day. Cliff watched TV on one bed while I worked with my Bible and notes all spread out on the other bed. He finally rolled over to sleep, and I promised him I'd join him soon.

About one in the morning, I'd finally finished. I was tired, but I felt good about what God wanted me to share with the ladies in the remaining two sessions. Ready to get in bed, I put my Bible down and closed my laptop and swung my legs over to leave that bed and tiptoe my way around to the other side of the bed where Cliff was sleeping.

But I'd forgotten these beds were higher than normal, and when I stepped down, I stepped too short and tripped, throwing me toward the closest thing in front of me—my poor husband, completely and soundly asleep.

"*What!*"

Cliff shot up and jumped out of bed, pushing me to the floor. I'd almost given him a heart attack. And I started giggling and couldn't stop.

"I'm so sorry!" I said, in between heaves of laughter.

Cliff tried to get his breath back as he slowly sat back down on the bed and looked at me out of one eye that was barely open. "Just come get in bed," he said. "Before you kill me."

The sessions on Saturday went smoothly. I was grateful for Andrew and Laremy leading worship, and I prayed hard for what God might do in the lives of the ladies there. At lunchtime, I got to sit with a sweet wife named Jennifer, who had two children, a boy and a girl, under age six. Her son had muscular dystrophy; her daughter was autistic. Jennifer was struggling. She was angry and her heart was breaking for her children and she could not understand why God would give her children the challenges that he had.

As a mama, my heart hurt with her. We talked and prayed, and I promised to connect her with another mama I know whose son had lived with muscular dystrophy for many years. I told her I was grateful she'd come.

I always like to end the last session with a question-and-answer time. I think it helps when we hear other people ask the same questions that have been on our own hearts, and it also helps when we hear others answer from their own experiences. The ladies asked some good questions, and then one of the wives shared that her husband never wants to write, and because phone calls come so infrequently from where he's deployed in Afghanistan, she was very worried that they would lose all sense of closeness while he was gone. What could she do?

I saw Cliff standing in the back with the other guys, looking down at an iPad, no doubt watching the LSU game that I knew was on at the moment, and I smiled.

"You know, I think this question could use some guy perspective, so I'm going to put my husband on the spot and ask him to come and answer," I said. "Cliff? Can you come here a second?"

Cliff gave me a "what are you doing?" look as he came and stood next to me, and I smiled big and gave him a quick recap of the wife's question.

"Well, first thing you have to realize is that you and your husband may communicate very differently," Cliff said, looking at the wife, who was sitting in the front row. "I know for Sara and me, she wants to sit down for hour-long conversations and write out our goals and dreams for the next fifty years."

I started giggling and Cliff noticed. He knew me so well.

"That's right, I'm spilling all your secrets," he said, smiling. The ladies laughed.

"For a lot of guys when they're over there, every day feels just like the day before. There may not be a whole lot of exciting stuff to talk about. But I know you still want to talk. I would ask your husband if he can write out a list of questions for you that you can answer and send back to him. That way, he's hearing about what you're doing, and then you can maybe ask him some questions, and maybe he can share that way as well."

As Cliff continued talking, I stood there, smiling, proud of him as I listened and watched the ladies respond to what he was saying. It felt so good standing there together. And that's when I realized something. That my prayer so many years ago—asking God to open the door so that Cliff could be involved in ministry with me—had just been answered. I think I have started to see what it looks like to "love *his* way"—to honor my husband, to be intentional in how I show love toward him, and to also be selfless. Responsibilities will still be there. Tasks may still require completion. But I *can* be submissive to my husband by putting him first in my attitude, in my love.

As with anything worth loving or doing, it isn't perfect. I think I'm going to mess up more than I succeed with this. But I also believe I'm seeing some of the blessings that come with stepping back and letting my husband lead. I'm excited to see what's ahead.

Do You Love Me Too?

This morning as I scrambled eggs and poured orange juice into glasses, the morning show hosts on the Christian radio station I listen to were discussing an interesting topic. They were talking about a recent study that questioned the meaning behind the second "I love you." You know, when your spouse tells you "I love you" as you're sitting on the couch watching television or you're talking on the phone together and you say "I love you" right before you hang up—the typical response from the other spouse is, "I love you too."

But there's a problem, say the experts. Saying "I love you too" just doesn't seem to count as much. It's too automated, it's too easily done without thinking. No, the experts say we should say "thank you" and leave it at that.

Really?

Cliff walked into the room and I told him what I'd just heard.

"What do you think about that?" I asked him as I handed him his plate of eggs with a little piece of toast on the side.

"I don't know," he said, digging into his breakfast. He looked up at me with that sparkle in his eyes. "Tell me you love me."

"I love you," I said, looking at him.

"Thanks," he said, looking at me.

We both laughed. That was so lame.

We say "I love you" to each other so many times in a day that I really can't count how often. Nor do I try to keep track. We say it in the morning when we wake up, and maybe when we're brushing our teeth; we say it in texts during the day and on the phone if we get a chance to chat. We say it when we see each other just before dinner gets put on the table, and we say it as we go to sleep at night. But we never really say the whole "I love you–I love you too" combination. We just say "I love you."

He loves me.

I love him.

We love each other. And saying it reminds us. It reminds us when we're irritated at each other or distracted with other things. Saying "I love you" re-rights us, like an ever careful nudge to make sure the valuable gift that is ours to watch over doesn't topple and get away from us. "I love yous" keep the foundation intact, the cracks a little less noticeable, or maybe a little less likely to spread.

Saying "Thank you" in response just takes that love and keeps it. But repeating those words…well, I'm giving that love back so it's given and received.

That's the way it should be.

When Husbands Don't Help

It's the beginning of November and I am on the road again, this time driving back to our old stomping grounds in Nashville. The biggest faith-based conference in the world for military wives is later this week, and I'm excited to teach a couple of workshops for it. But I'm sad Cliff couldn't come with me. He's staying behind to make sure Caleb stays focused in school.

As I said previously, I've tried hard for a couple of years now to include Cliff in what I do. It probably all started when he was laid off from his job six months after he got back from his first deployment. I liked the idea of us working together. But our working styles are very, very different. Different can be good, but it can also take some work and some time to get used to.

I'm wondering this year, though, as I work harder to put him first in our marriage and our family, if I should not also give him respect and priority when it comes to what I do. In my ministry, in my writing, in my job. He likes to help when he can, and I find I tend to become one-track minded when I'm pursuing a project on my own, to the point of being oblivious to everything around me. It's something I have to fight against constantly, and I've seen improvements in myself since the Proverbs 31 experiment, but I know there are still things I'm sorting out. When Cliff steps in and helps, it reminds me that I have a team, and I'm not just on my own.

This week he offered to help create some listening guides I wanted to provide for my classes, and I gratefully agreed. But by the time I was ready to get on the road for the eight-hour drive, they were still not quite done. No problem, thanks to the beauty of technology. He would keep working on them, email the files to me, and I'd just take them to the local quick printing place before I headed to the hotel where the conference would be. Plus, I was driving up two days early for some meetings and to visit with a friend, so there should be plenty of time.

And yet, Thursday came and there I sat, at a corner table at Panera's, trying not to tap my fingers in impatience as I stared at my laptop. Cliff still wasn't done with the guides. And I had less than two hours to take them to get printed and head over to the hotel and a meeting, which was on the other side of Nashville. During rush hour. My odds of making the meeting on time were looking less and less likely.

I checked with him one more time. Still working, he texted. Sorry, he said.

I really wanted to value my husband's work and his effort. I wanted to respect it. But the deadline was here.

I quickly opened a software program and went to work. In thirty minutes, I had my listening guides. I was looking up directions to the printer when I got another text from Cliff.

I'M ALMOST DONE.

I texted back, feeling a little guilty. "That's OK, I went ahead and did them." I told him where he could look in the Dropbox folder we shared to see them.

"Wow," he texted back. "They look great."

As he looked up the number and called the printer for me while I saved the files onto a thumb drive and prepared to dash out to my car, I thought about what had just happened.

I'd depended on Cliff to get something done that, really, I was a lot more suited for. It was more in my area of strength. And yet, trying to be submissive, I'd put more pressure on both of us than we'd needed.

Backward thinking?

Does being submissive mean also being submissive when it comes to career, when it comes to job, when it comes to just practical, "let's get 'er done" tasks? I mean, can you insist the wife cook even when she burns boiled water and the family may just actually starve? What if the husband, as hard as he tries, really struggles to find a good job?

I'm not so sure. What about the talents and gifts God gives each of us as husband and wife? I've always believed God often puts spouses together who are opposites, or who have different strengths and weaknesses than the person they married. It's a beautiful example of the harmony a marriage can offer.

I don't think God's plan of submission involves some twisted version of *The Stepford Wives* where the women are robots and the men are free to reign as they choose. And yet, as women eager to follow God's design, we might tend to err on that side if we're not careful. For some of us, it might just be easier to be that way.

But I'm not sure God designed us as wives to be yes-women to our husbands. Otherwise, where does the whole "iron sharpening iron" thing happen? No, God did not create us to be robots, and while Eve was fashioned from Adam's rib, we are still made in God's image—not Adam's. Not man's. We may have been formed from man, but we are still God's creation (Genesis 5:1-2). As wives, we have purpose, we have a role that's greatly important, but I also don't think it's our only role, our only purpose.

Maybe the point is how we keep it all in the right order. And maybe that requires right perspective. I'm still learning this.

I had a lot of time to think on my drive home after my trip. Part of the way I spent listening to an audiobook version of *Not a Fan* by Kyle Idleman. It's an incredible book that outlines the distinctions between just being a fan of Jesus and actually being a follower. I so want to live out what I believe. In everything I do—in my ministry and in my marriage.

But I continue to struggle with all of it, more so than I prefer to admit sometimes. I love doing ministry—I love writing and hearing when God uses something I wrote to encourage someone else, maybe even into a deeper walk with him. I really enjoy speaking and encouraging wives that way.

I know Cliff is trying to be more present as a leader to our family and in our marriage. But sometimes his attempts feel like little shooting stars, and they stun me more than help me. I'm cruising along, keeping things going, maintaining organization and routine, and *bam!*, he steps in to lead and I'm thrown off, asking myself (though in a whisper), "*Now* you're leading?"

It seems to be easier to be submissive when he appears to be doing more of the work or carrying more of the weight. Like a dance, where he's leading and I'm following. Though come to think of it, we have not danced that much in our fourteen years of marriage, and at times when we have, I've been a really bad follower.

Which probably says something very profound right there.

It's harder to feel submissive when we both are doing equal tasks or seemingly equal roles, or the scales have turned and I'm leading point on something and he's supporting me or backing me up.

Perhaps the secret is accepting his flaws and admitting my own.

Maybe when I want to point out what he might not be doing as our leader, I should instead focus what I could do to be more of a helper.

Saturday morning we were working on cleaning up the house and putting away the laundry when I decided, as we slowly near the end of this whole experiment, to ask Cliff the question he hates. But it has to be asked because it's necessary for my "heart wants to know" inquisitiveness.

"Have you seen a difference during this year? Are you seeing changes in me?" I asked him, my eyes quite serious as I sit down on the edge of the bed.

He looked at me and smiled, but not before rolling his eyes first. He will never be able to avoid my inquisitive (obsessive) questions.

But he thought for a minute before he spoke.

"Yes, I've seen changes," he said. "Yes, I've seen a difference. You think more about asking me before you do something. You seem to give me more time to think about a decision before you rush off and make one."

"Well," I said, "I know I've seen changes in you. You've really stepped up in a lot of ways leading our family that maybe wasn't there a few years ago."

Then he said something that made the entire last twelve months absolutely worth it.

"Well, I realize now that one of the reasons it's good for me to step up as leader is because you're a worrier, and it's not always good for the worrier to make major decisions."

He started walking out of the room to get more clean laundry. I looked after him as if he'd just told me he knew the code to winning the million-dollar prize from McDonald's Monopoly.

"Thank you! Finally!" I blurted and threw my hands in the air before I could stop myself.

Yes! I know I'm more emotional. I know I can be a serious worrier. So much so that it can freeze me up and pin me down. And I have so wanted—make that yearned—for Cliff to one day realize that and make more of an effort to take some of that weight off me. But I wasn't always willing to let it go either.

He glanced back at me in amused annoyance at my response.

"Sorry," I said, "but I just totally 100 percent agree. And I love you for it."

My heart felt a little lighter just then. And a whole lot freer.

I called my friend Heather later and told her about our conversation, as well as to check on her. Overnight, a serious storm had blown through, and her neighborhood had gotten the brunt of it, with wind so strong it actually blew out her garage door. She'd posted pictures on Facebook, and I wanted to make sure she and her family were OK.

When I told her what Cliff had said, she responded, "Yes, I know exactly what you mean! Andre was on the phone with the insurance company this morning, and they were saying it would be at least a week before they could get out here to do an estimate of the damage. I've never heard my husband get as mad as he did on the phone with them! Usually I'm the one that has to be the bad guy, or I'm in the background hissing through my teeth, 'Tell them *this*' or 'You need to say *that*.' But I just kept quiet and listened, and I'll be honest, I really liked it. I felt happy listening to him defend our needs and handle that problem. It kinda surprised me, but I liked it."

I wonder if we women spend so much time fighting to hold on to what everyone else has told us we need to hold on to that we're missing out on the freedom that comes with letting go. And our husbands miss out on the blessing of leading in the way God's called them to.

Finding My Happy Place

It's occurred to me that the week we're about to start may very well be a final exam, of sorts, for this year's lessons in exploring what it means to be submissive to my husband.

We're going on a family vacation.

To Disney World.

With a mix of family members and friends of family—eighteen of us staying in a condo.

I'm a little scared. Because let's just be a little realistic about this whole imaginative place we've all deemed dreamlike and enchanting. Disney may call itself the Happiest Place on Earth, but anyone who's actually been can agree that between babies crying, kids whining, and parents snapping, "No, I'm *not* buying you anything else!"—there is reasonable risk for major meltdowns.

And now my type A self is going to follow my type B husband into this place.

Follow.

As in, let him lead.

And more precisely—let him and others lead.

We've been several times, a couple of trips with family and a couple just with us, usually after Cliff's come home from his deployments.

This particular trip has been planned for almost a full year. But there are a whole lot of changing variables. What started out as a family vacation with just family coming from different parts of the country has now morphed into some family staying home and some friends of certain family members and acquaintances coming along, people we really don't know very well, and who really don't know us.

Though we've been promised a nice room with a queen-size bed, we're arriving later than everyone else because Cliff has had an unexpected navy training come up that he cannot miss, and plans still feel a little uncertain. We're sending Caleb ahead by a few days with the rest of the family so he won't miss out on any of the fun, but he's also going to be with some friends of cousins who are coming along who haven't always been nice to him.

It's made things just a tad stressful. Which, you know, is normal for vacations with extended family, right?

I'm trying not to worry about all of those issues. Instead, I'm attempting to just focus on letting my husband lead, and me being the one who follows. Of course, at the moment, this feels a bit like being led to the gallows when I think about all that might go wrong in the next seven days, but you have to go sometime. My time may just be now.

I decided I could still help by doing some research, and I found some online planning tools for the trip, which I passed on to Cliff. One handy little software program does a great job planning out where and when to go in the parks, and which parks will have the lightest crowds each day. (Look, I want to be submissive, but I also don't want to stand in line for two hours. A girl has her limits.)

Cliff was impressed and shared it with the rest of the family. And though none of them will look at it again, probably, Cliff said we would. And that was good enough for me.

Caleb left with the others on Friday. That morning, I once again wished we were all going at the same time, but Cliff couldn't go until Monday since he was already in Shreveport for his training, and I needed the extra couple of days to work on my writing project. So on Friday I checked Caleb out of school early to join the others on their drive down to Florida. Caleb was excited. I was still a little nervous.

Mamaw had broken her hip the week before and had just been released from the hospital, so Ms. Nancy was staying home with her. Everyone met at her house, though, to load up the luggage and start the caravan of cars that would be driving down. After good-byes all around, and watching them finally drive away, I took a deep breath. There was nothing else I could do now. It was out of my control. All I could do was just hope everything went smoothly and that Caleb would have a great time until we got there.

By the time Cliff got home just after six on Sunday night, I was ready to leave. Besides writing, I'd cleaned the entire house from top to bottom and put all the Christmas decorations out and in place, including the tree. Just one box of special ornaments was left that I saved for Cliff and Caleb to put up when we all got back from the trip. I'd cleaned out the car, topped it off with gas, pulled out our suitcases, and made sure the dog was set with food and treats. If this wasn't helping, I didn't know what was.

My mom was housesitting for us, and she and I were back in my bedroom talking when Cliff arrived. While Mom hung out in the game room and watched television with the dog, Cliff and I finished packing. I was dying for him to say something about the house—how great it looked, how pretty the decorations were—but he didn't say anything. Probably hadn't noticed. Men and their one-track minds. I understood, though, that he'd just driven half a day from his drill weekend, so I tried not to care.

There was just one thing left I had to grab. My fanny pack.

That's right, judge all you want. Call it a belt bag or a belt purse. But this little bag and I have a history, and I like taking it to places like big crazy amusement parks where I don't have to tote a heavy purse (that everyone else ends up throwing their stuff into).

I bought the fanny pack in the airport in Amsterdam during a layover on a trip I took with a photographer named Jim to cover the first week of the Iraq War on board an aircraft carrier. He'd noticed all I had was my backpack and suggested I might want something smaller for carrying my cash and passport. So we went browsing, and I found this black-leather fanny pack, er, belt bag. Apparently, it was a designer label, because I walked out of the store not just with a fanny pack but an eighty-dollar fanny pack. That's right, people, this southern girl knows how to style.

Seriously. Eighty dollars. The thing will be willed to somebody when I die.

For almost ten years I've held on to it, and it looks pretty much like the day I bought it. But Cliff hates it. Always has. And now, I couldn't find it.

"Cliff," I called from our bedroom and walked quickly down the hall to where he was standing in the kitchen. "Have you seen my fanny pack?"

He threw me a glance. And a smirk.

"Yes."

"Where's my fanny pack?" I threw him a look back. Not a very nice one.

"You don't need your fanny pack."

"I do need my fanny pack. I like to have it with me when we go to the parks."

"I've got my backpack. You can put your stuff in there."

"*Where* is my fanny pack? It's not like it's bright orange or rainbow colored or neon green. It's black leather. It's stylish…in its own way. And I like using it."

"Yes," Cliff said. "I agree. It's very nice. It's fine, hand-stitched Italian leather *ruined* by making it into a fanny pack."

I glared at him.

"Sara, it's for old ladies. And you are not old."

I looked at his face. Cliff isn't stubborn about a lot of things, but this was one thing he was putting his foot down on. Seriously. Over a fanny pack.

Is this where submission was required? My husband, saying yes or no to my fashion statements? I'm pretty sure nowhere in the Bible does it say, "Men, honor your wives by keeping their fanny packs at home."

I took a deep breath and looked at my husband's face.

"Head of household," he mouthed. And smiled.

I wanted to smack him.

Mom walked into the kitchen. "Are ya'll about ready?" she asked.

"Cliff won't let me take my fanny pack," I told her.

"He won't *let* you?" my mom said, her tone bordering on shrill, her eyes shooting me a look.

"He doesn't want me taking it. He doesn't like it." I felt tears forming at the corner of my eyes. For real. I was going to cry over a fanny pack.

I looked back at Cliff, who knew he'd won. This time.

"Fine," I said. "But you're carrying everything in your backpack. And I don't want to hear one word about it when I stop you fifty times to pull out my lip balm or my wallet or anything else I think of."

(As I said this, I secretly considered stuffing in dozens of feminine hygiene products just on principle. "Honey," I could say, in the middle of two hundred people lined up for Rock 'n' Rollercoaster, "can you pass me a tampon?")

"That's fine," Cliff said, and bent down to give me a peck on the lips.

I kissed him back, but not without a well-measured roll of the eyes.

"I cannot believe you won't let me bring my fanny pack," I muttered as we started pulling suitcases toward the car.

Once we were finally ready to get on the road, it was after seven p.m. Since he'd driven four hours already, I volunteered to drive. I was tired and I'm not a night person at all, but I wanted to do it to help him. Thirty minutes into our trip, though, just as we reached Baton Rouge, we realized neither one of us had eaten dinner.

"What are you in the mood for?" Cliff asked.

"Pancakes," I said, suddenly inspired for breakfast. "Can we go to IHOP?"

Cliff looked out the window. "How about Illegal Burritos?"

Seriously. 'Cause that's like pancakes.

I kept my mouth shut. I was going to let him decide. But I really wished he would listen to me. There weren't too many times when we talked about meals that I had a specific wish. And being the navigationally challenged person I am, I had no idea where IHOP or any other restaurant was unless Cliff led me there.

And I wanted pancakes. Without the salsa. And he stole my fanny pack.

Ten minutes later, Cliff was directing me to an IHOP. We were seated at a booth by the window and both of us ordered pancakes-and-eggs combinations. As he was telling me about his weekend at drill, a young guy, probably in his late twenties, walked into the dining area. He stopped in front of our table.

"Excuse me, folks, sorry to bother you, but I've locked my keys in my car and I need some cash to pay the Pop-A-Lock guy who's gonna be here in about ten minutes. Can you help me out?"

I looked at Cliff. In this instance, I was happy to let him be the decision maker. Lead away, my husband.

Cliff pulled out his wallet. All he had was a five-dollar bill, which he handed over to the guy. Out of the seven tables in there, I noticed we were the only ones who gave him anything. I love my husband.

After a fun dinner, or rather breakfast, we walked out into the brisk air and headed for the car. Cliff noticed a coffee shop across the street and people sitting outside, sipping on their hot drinks. He joked, as he put his arm around me and guided me through the parking lot, "That guy better not be over there drinking a latte or I'm asking for my money back."

Cliff slept most of the way to Alabama, where we planned on stopping for the night. The last hour, I felt miserable. My legs and back were cramping from staying up until two the night before scrubbing bathroom and kitchen floors. I was more than ready to get to the hotel when we finally pulled in around midnight.

Cliff had booked the hotel using points he'd earned while traveling for his job over the summer. It was a free night's stay, so I should have just been happy with that. But I'm picky when it comes to hotels. I don't like icky. And as we walked into the room, this was bordering on icky.

The carpet looked dirty. The bed looked OK. The floor had some weird bumpiness to it, like there were sinkholes forming. I felt as if I were walking over miniature hills when I crossed the room.

"Um, did you read reviews?" I asked as I peered into the tiny bathroom.

Cliff was tired and already getting under the covers. "Yes, they were OK. It's one night."

This from the guy who sleeps on the ground in nothing but a sleeping bag with his Kevlar vest as a pillow. Yes, it was one night. And it was free. I kept my mouth shut and gave him a big smile as I climbed in next to him and tried not to think how clean the sheets were or weren't.

We didn't sleep much thanks to the bright light radiating just underneath the curtain. It was so bright, Cliff thought it was daylight when he woke me up to say good morning. I checked my phone. It was five a.m. Then his mom texted him thirty minutes later. My second night in a row of four hours of sleep.

I kept my mouth shut.

We packed up and headed back out to the car. I was looking forward to Cliff driving and getting a little rest. Until he said, "Why don't you drive the first half, and I'll drive when we get closer to Orlando?"

Great. Yes, why couldn't I do that?

My back and legs started protesting as soon as I sat behind the wheel.

As I pulled the car once again onto the interstate, I wrestled with myself inside. This submission stuff is frustrating at times. Cliff had his seat laid back, playing on his phone. I was bored out of my mind driving, so I played with the radio.

I thought about some of the things that had happened over the last couple of months and how I'd intentionally started stepping back when it came to minor disagreements or problems with family. In a way, it did feel a little freeing to let Cliff handle things with his family, instead of me trying to be the one. I suppose that tendency just came from watching my parents growing up. My dad had very little communication with his family, and it was my mother who made the phone calls and sent the letters and kept up with my dad's father and his siblings.

I think as wives we can worry a lot about our husbands' families. We probably try to control how they behave as much as we sometimes try to control our husbands. But how's that really working? So I'm trying to release all that. When it comes down to it, I probably worry most about it because I worry about what they think of me, and that anything negative will be reflected back on me, the wife. And I want them to like me.

I realize, though, after fourteen years of marriage, I'm still wanting them to like me. And I'm still not always sure they do. So while Cliff is playing on his iPhone and I'm hunched over the steering wheel, trying to pray away the spasms in my shoulder blades, I'm thinking that I'm not going to worry about that so much anymore. Because I can only be me. And I think there comes a point where I have to recognize his relationship with his family and his relationship with me are two different relationships. And it's not my job to control or be in charge of both. It's my job to support him. And if supporting him means honoring and being kind to his family, then by all means, I'll do it. But I'm also going to follow his lead first.

Then my phone rang. It was a close friend of mine who had heard some bad news. A couple we've both known for a long time just separated. The wife was having an affair with someone she worked with and left the marriage. By the time I got off the phone, I was in tears.

I don't understand how people can just walk away from their marriages. This couple married the same year we did. We're not close anymore and really only see them in passing these days, but my heart still hurts to see someone just give up like that. To walk away from fourteen years of commitment.

Cliff and I talked about it, and he reminded me that we didn't know the entire story. I agree with him, I know he's right, but it still makes me sad. I'm sad for marriages in general right now. Because I know the story I just heard isn't the first time this year I've heard it, nor will it probably be the last. There are many military marriages I know about that haven't made it.

The tears rolled down my face as I studied the road in front of me and I tried to put into words what I was thinking.

"When I think about the ups and downs we've had as a couple, I know there were probably times that we could have given up or walked away, but we didn't," I said. "We haven't. We keep going. We work through the junk, we talk through the problems. I can't imagine you not in my life. I can't imagine walking away from all that we've been through together, the good and the bad, but especially the bad—because it's the bad that's helped get us to where we are today, don't you think?"

I don't know if I made any sense, but my heart was grasping for the right words to describe what I felt. The bad cuts away the fluff.

We drove by some fields on our right, and I thought about what cotton looks like. The cotton part of the cotton plant is soft, but trying to get to that part can hurt—literally. Cotton bolls are sharp and can cut your fingers and hands and make them bleed.

In life, there is so much fluff. But marriage has a way of honing down that fluff into a solid foundation that can't be stripped, but it takes time to build. Sometimes, it takes pain to build. But once it's built, it can stand. I don't expect the foundation of our marriage to be finished for a long, long time. But I'm committed to doing everything I can to help make it solid.

I think about all the great qualities my husband has—he is kind and gentle and, of course, he's funny. He makes me laugh every day. He has a patience within him that I can only wish I had a piece of. I think about how much he's grown this year, how much I've grown this year. But it's taken work. It's taken commitment. It's taken being intentional. And it certainly isn't easy.

But it's worth it. It is so, so worth it.

We stopped for lunch at a Krystal Burger, and as we sat down at the table, Cliff once again brought up the love conversation we've had several times the last few weeks. The one about the study that says it's not necessarily good to say "I love you too" when someone says "I love you."

"Tell me you love me," he said, sitting across from me, smiling big.

"I love you," I said, smiling back.

"I'm glad."

I laughed and rolled my eyes. An older man with white hair at a table next to us looked over and smiled.

I said it again, a little quieter. "I love you."

"Uh-huh," he said.

"Now you say it," I told him.

"I love you," he said.

"Can I have a fry?" I asked, as I grabbed one off his tray.

He said mine wasn't nearly as funny as his. I disagree.

Cliff drove the rest of the way as he promised, and we finally reached Orlando around dinner time. Since we knew everyone was still at the park, we made our way to Downtown Disney for some dinner and window shopping. It was nice to just walk around together and have a little time to ourselves. The last couple of months have been stressful and busy, and it felt good to just slow down a little. We looked at Christmas ornaments and browsed through stores, and Cliff found a T-shirt sporting Walt Disney's head. He decided he might buy the shirt if he saw it again later in the week.

Even though we couldn't get in touch with anyone who was already set up at the house, we decided to leave and make our way there. First, we stopped at a grocery store for some microwave sausage biscuits for breakfast, about thirty minutes out of our way. I don't think Cliff will rely on me again for directions. Tired and ready to just crash and unwind after a long few days, we finally got to the house about nine thirty. We had the access code, and so we figured we'd at least find our room and get unpacked before the rest of them got back.

I only wish it had gone that way.

Let's just say our experience with the condo and our accommodations didn't quite live up to our expectations. That my disappointment with some things and the feeling "we got gypped" quickly swelled to anger, and poor Cliff was the one who got to hear it. Because he was the only one around to hear it.

Enough said.

I was ashamed at how angry I got. How I flew off the handle, even if only Cliff and God had seen it. I realized I'd failed my final exam before it had really even started, and it made me sad. And later that night I told Cliff.

He listened and took my hand.

"I get it, Sara, I do," he said. "I feel let down too. I don't know why it's worked out the way it has, why things haven't gone how we expected they would. But here's what we're going to do. Tomorrow morning, we're getting up and we're going to go have fun with Caleb. We're not going to worry about what anyone else is doing. We're just going to go have some fun."

His eyes looked wet. "The whole reason I agreed to this trip in the first place was so we could have some time with family since I won't be here next year. That's what I wanted, that's why we came. But my family is you and Caleb. That's who comes first. And so we're going to make the best of what this is, and we're going to enjoy being together."

I felt bad. I hadn't thought about the fact that Cliff wouldn't be here for Thanksgiving and Christmas next year. I guess I hadn't let myself think that far ahead. I vowed to myself to get over a disappointing first night, and I rested my head against Cliff's shoulder, just thankful to be with him at all.

Some battles just don't matter.

We woke up bright and early Tuesday morning. The house was quiet. Everyone else was upstairs, still sleeping. They weren't planning on getting to the parks until later. Caleb was now sleeping on a twin mattress laid out at the end of our bed. He'd been more than ready to see us get there. Though I still felt tinges of heaviness around my heart with all the disappointment from the night before, I tried hard to shake it off. Cliff was taking lead, and I was supposed to be helping. And we were going to have a good day.

Turns out we did have a good day. Caleb rode the Rock 'n' Roller-coaster for his first time ever, and thanks to the handy-dandy little app

I'd found online, there was no ride we stood in line for longer than fifteen minutes.

And that's how it was the rest of the week. The three of us would wake
up early and get to the park when it opened and come home when the
park closed. We did a couple of meals with everyone together (which is
always interesting when there's eighteen people to sit) and a couple of
shows like Fantasmic!, but for the most part we did our own thing. And
while I felt twinges of guilt at times about it, Cliff didn't. And I tried to
be OK with it too.

Thursday afternoon, we met up with some other friends who were
also in town for Disney. They have a daughter Caleb's age that he's good
friends with, and we hung out with them through the end of Friday night.
We had a blast.

Sometime during the week, when Cliff and I were walking by ourselves, I told him again how sorry I was about my attitude at the beginning of our trip and how the week had started off.

"I'm sorry I just didn't shut up and listen to you and keep my cool and
not get so angry," I told him.

He held my hand a little tighter and looked at me. "Sara, here's the
thing. Christ never asks us to be perfect in following him, he just asks us
to follow him. We're going to mess up. Because we have flaws.

"Your experiment with the Proverbs 31 wife wasn't perfect, as I remember," he said, smiling, wrapping one arm around my shoulder and pulling me in. "But you tried and you learned. This submission thing isn't any
different. You're not going to do it perfectly, but the point is you try. I'm
not always great at being the leader of our family. But I'm trying. We learn
from when we fail, and we keep going."

I knew he was right, and I really appreciated the reminder that this
whole thing isn't a pursuit of perfection but just a pursuit of the process.
And I think it is a process. I don't think you can wake up with a submissive heart to God and to your husband overnight. Maybe if God places
it on your heart and actively changes you in a moment. But I think for
most of us this has to be an attitude that's learned. Like my desire to be a

great wife and mom to my family. Those things that help me do that better today were not things that came naturally to me two years ago. It took time and it took intentionality. I don't think submission is any different.

I also think the biggest area I failed in this whole Happiest Place on Earth episode was that I didn't pray. I didn't pray before the trip, I didn't pray in the midst of the trip, and I didn't pray after it either. I was so wrapped up in my own energies, my own attempts to fix and solve, my own attempts (however weak) to control, that I forgot the most basic solution of all.

Letting it go and giving it to God. And that starts with prayer.

The end of the week finally arrived, and the house was picked up and belongings packed up and everyone started to leave. It was fun, it was exhausting, it was frustrating. It was indeed educational. And it's a week, for different reasons than most, I probably won't forget any time soon.

And maybe that's a good thing.

His Helper

For the last several months, Cliff's shoulder has bothered him to the point where he can no longer lift his arm without causing an incredible sharp pain.

"So don't lift your arm," I tell him, helpfully.

He was not amused.

Actually, I was the one who kept telling him he needed to see a doctor. Cliff, like me, does not go to doctors "just because." He usually has to be deathly ill before that happens. He finally agreed to go, and his general doctor referred him to a specialist who ordered an MRI. The results showed a tear in his rotator cuff.

Ouch.

He has no idea where he did it or how it happened. My suspicion is that CrossFit has something to do with it, but Cliff is pleading the Fifth. Still, it means surgery and serious recovery time. The more I read about this surgery, the more I'm discovering it's difficult—not the surgery itself but the time required to heal.

And right before Christmas. And a book deadline.

Good times.

All of my research told me I should prepare some things ahead of time. Frozen meals are good, but nothing that'll require a knife to cut up. I spent two days preparing two weeks of meals. He's going to be the One-Armed Man for quite a while. He may need ice packs, so I bought these huge bags of frozen vegetables, which according to one blogger make the ideal ice-packs because they're flexible.

I also read that he's going to be spending a lot of time on the recliner. We don't have the traditional recliner, but we do have a love seat that reclines. When I mentioned to Cliff about maybe moving it into the game room, switching it out with our red chair that's in there, he didn't seem too concerned.

"It's no big deal. I'll just sleep in the living room."

Yes, because having him sleep in the central part of the house when Caleb still has school and I have to get him up and going, yes, that is the ideal thing to do.

Men. What would they do without us?

With his surgery just a few days away, I kissed him good-bye for a navy drill weekend he needed to leave early for, and after dropping Caleb off for school, I decided to go ahead and move the furniture so I didn't have to think about it later.

The red chair moved pretty easily. It's one of those chaise lounges, a thrift-store find Ms. Nancy came across one year on her way to see us in Nashville. She bought it for fifty dollars and figured if we didn't want it, she'd just take it home with her. We did. It's the most comfortable chair we own.

I got the red chair moved out into the living room and then set my attention on the love seat. This was a little trickier. Because it's a recliner, it's much bulkier and a lot heavier. Cliff told me before he left that he'd get his brother to come over and help later that night. But I thought back to how much furniture my mother moved in her day, and I told myself to suck it up and get 'er done.

Progress was being made until I got to the doorway of the game room. The weight of the couch was too heavy for me to prop it up vertically (I tried), so it was going to have to go through at an odd angle.

A little voice whispered in my head, *maybe you should ask for help*.

I ignored the voice because I wanted to get this couch into the room. I wanted to help my husband by having everything completely ready for him by the time his surgery got here, and I didn't want to wait on anyone else to come do it when I and my perfectly useable arms and legs should be able to get the job done.

That's what I thought, anyway.

But the interior wall just inside the doorway of the game room disagreed.

I forgot about the odd corner wall that sat two feet into the room until I'd already pushed and grunted and shoved the couch as much as I could from the outside, pretty much trapping it in place.

So I got smart. I found a way to climb over the couch and into the room. I would just pull the couch through. Because, of course, if pushing doesn't work, then pulling will.

I managed to pull the couch forward another inch. Just enough to get it stuck really good.

Stuck, meaning not budging. Not going anywhere. And blocking my one exit.

Now I had to contemplate my next option. And wonder if it could really be possible I might die in here. Trapped. My only exit to food, water, and, most important, bathroom denied by one really large recliner love seat, tipped on its side and mocking me.

You should have waited for some help.

I should have waited for some help.

I noticed Sammy looking at me through the one little space that was open in the doorway. Loyal to the end, he scrunched down on the floor and wriggled his oversized schnauzer mass through the hole and came over to me, where I sat in a corner of the pretty-much empty room, my back to the television. He stuck his warm nose to mine, no doubt to make sure I was still alive, and walked back to the doorway, where it was obvious, even to him, there was no way to get out. He lay down and looked back at me, as if to say, "You really should have waited for some help."

Yeah, yeah, and I don't see you doing anything helpful, I thought. *Lassie, you are not.*

I did do one thing right. In what was probably a vision of my stubborn stupidity, I had made a point to stick my phone in my back pocket. I took a picture of my blocked entrance and posted it on Facebook with a witty comment about clearly not thinking some things through.

No replies.

I really could die in here. Or maybe, more realistically, just wet my pants.

I stretched out on the carpet, gazing up at the ceiling fan that really did need dusting, and thought about where Cliff was at the moment. Half-way to Mississippi probably. Caleb needed to be picked up at school in six hours. So at least by then someone might notice I was gone.

Like other weary travelers who find themselves stuck in weird places by heavy pieces of furniture, I pondered what got me here.

I didn't ask for help.

OK, let's be a little more clear. I refused to ask for help.

But the million-dollar answer...

I didn't want to wait.

Being willing to wait is probably a characteristic I should include with being submissive. Cliff doesn't always make decisions as fast as I do, or as fast as I would like. He doesn't always move as fast as I would like. He takes more time with things. It's probably one reason he's so much better at wrapping presents than I am. He takes his time, trims off the extra, folds down the ends, makes everything nice and neat. Sometimes my wrapped presents look like my son wrapped them. Which I am all too eager sometimes to say he did. I don't like taking the time. I don't like waiting.

But there is good that comes in waiting, isn't there?

I think back to poor Eve. She didn't wait, did she? She didn't ask Adam his thoughts before eating what the snake offered her. She just ate it. Maybe if she would have waited, maybe if she would have talked to Adam first, the two of them could have had a conversation that went something like this:

> *Eve*: "So, Adam, honey, this nice snake over here says that the fruit God told us we shouldn't eat is actually pretty yummy. What do you think?"
>
> *Adam*: "Well, babe, I don't know. I mean, God was pretty clear about that fruit. And there is so much of everything else we can eat. And besides, since when do you talk to snakes?"
>
> *Eve*: "Well, just for the record, he started talking to me first. You don't have to be so jealous, Adam. But you're right, God did sound pretty firm about that one fruit. I was just really curious about what it tasted like."
>
> *Adam*: "Terrible."
>
> *Eve*: "How do you know?"
>
> *Adam* (nuzzling her neck): "Because you're the sweetest piece of fruit around here."
>
> *Eve*: "Oh, Adam…" (giggling as they walk off, away from the fruit and the creepy snake with the demon-possessed eyes).

I let go of my Adam/Eve scenario and stood up, trying to figure out what I should do in that moment. The couch blocking my way was a pretty good indicator I was still really bad at waiting. Even if I had good intentions. There really was no reason I couldn't have waited for help.

Picking Sammy up, I gently hoisted him over the chair and back into freedom. My exit was a little more difficult. The only way over was to climb, and I held my breath, hoping I wasn't so heavy I'd end up breaking the arm of the couch. Because that would be a fun story to have to tell Cliff. Your wife was so dumb she shoved a couch into the door and got it stuck, and then she was so heavy, she broke it trying to get out.

I gingerly climbed on top of the couch and carefully lowered myself down the other side.

My mom called a little while later, and I told her about my dumb mistake and how I'm going to have to get Clay or a couple of guys to move it for me.

"Psssh, whatever, I'm coming over after work and I bet we can get it in there. We don't need men to do it!"

Stubborn is genetic in my family, apparently.

Mom showed up after I picked up Caleb from school. After taking a look and giving the couch one little shove, she stepped back.

"Yeah, you've got it stuck, all right. I would have tried going in from the other side, turning the couch around this way," she said, pointing to the spine of the couch that's on the right, and motioning to her left.

"Yeah, I didn't think about that," I said, thinking that didn't really help at this moment.

We wondered if we could take the couch apart to bring it in piecemeal. I grabbed a screwdriver and we started looking underneath. I suddenly envisioned taking apart the entire couch and then not being able to put it back together.

"Um, I think I probably just need to wait for Clay."

My mother agreed, her "women can do anything men can do" voice more subdued now. Clearly, I have not completely learned her ways.

Several hours later, Clay came by at Cliff's request to help with the couch. He was able to take off the back of the couch the way they had to do it when they moved us into the house in March. Um, I apparently didn't see that part. And that was so much easier, I have to say.

When Cliff got home at the end of his drill weekend, the room was all ready. The love seat looked good in there, and I'd fixed up a little side table complete with lamp, box of tissues, basket of hard candy, lotion, the TV remote, and what really impressed him—an electric outlet strip that will let him plug in his iPad and his iPhone.

I realized the man may never leave once he gets in there. But it felt good to do what I could for him.

Surgery was two days later. After we dropped Caleb off at school, we pulled up to the hospital at 7:15 a.m., the time we were supposed to show up. Cliff's mom's SUV was already in the parking lot.

We checked in with the nurse and made our way into the pre-op area. Cliff went off somewhere at the bidding of a nurse, and just a minute later his mom stuck her head around the door and saw me.

"There you are!" She said it like we were late for a party. But I had to do a double take. One side of Ms. Nancy's face looked like play dough that lost a fight with a toddler. It was all slanting down.

"Um, Ms. Nancy, are you OK?" Knowing her, she could have been having a stroke at the moment and ignoring it.

She sighed a big sigh. "I was hoping no one would notice. I have a tooth infection."

The woman is seriously an Energizer Bunny. Because who else would come in from a trip late the night before, with a massive tooth infection that has made its way into her jaw, and still show up before us for her son's surgery?

"And why are you here?" I asked, a concerned look on my face.

"He's my baby," she said, smiling, which I'm sure was also an attempt to hide the wince from the pain in her mouth.

I hugged her and told her how glad I was that she was here. This was the first time Cliff had ever faced anything worse than the flu. It wasn't life-threatening, of course, but I knew it was getting ready to take him out of commission for several days. And I knew it was up to me to help him.

There's that word again. *Help.* I am his helper. It's starting to wear on me—not in a bad way, like the way a tire wears down, but in a good way… like the comforting feel of my long, knitted, grey cardigan sweater I love to pull around me when I want to feel warm and nestled and safe.

I looked at Cliff as he was answering the nurse's pre-op questions, and I wondered—my handsome husband whom I rely on so much, the smile on his face that still brings a smile to mine, the joy I still get at just seeing him walk into a room—do I feel that way to him? Can he see me in that way? Does he see me like that? Warm and comforting and safe? I want to help more than hinder; I want to encourage more than criticize. I want to love him with everything I have, to return what I often feel from him. I want to be his helper.

A final kiss, one last assurance from the nurse he would be just fine, and Ms. Nancy and I walked our way over to the outpatient waiting room. I had considered bringing my laptop to do some work while Cliff was in surgery, but as we settled down in chairs, I was glad I hadn't. This is a small town, after all, and small towns bring many visitors.

The first to arrive was Dr. Barnes, who served as the pastor of our church for over forty years. And even now, in retirement, he continues his hospital visits, usually getting there ahead of our current pastor and staff members. Even though he's in his seventies, his hair still has black to it, and he walks as purposefully and seriously now as he did when he was younger. He knows the halls and hospital room numbers instinctively and carries in his hand his little printout for the day, noting the names of people and loved ones of those he knows and even friends of friends of friends he might have met one day five years ago. Each one would get a visit and a short prayer before the morning was through. And then he would head to the hospitals in Baton Rouge. For him, ministry has never been just an occupation.

We smiled and exchanged hellos, and he asked for an update on Cliff. When he found out he'd already been taken back to get prepped—technically the place where no visitors were allowed—he left us for the moment. Because if there is one person you just don't say no to, it's Dr. Barnes. And God. And I'm pretty sure the hospital staff deem him one and the same at times.

While he was in the back with Cliff, our current pastor, Reggie, showed up and sat down with us. He's the same age as Cliff and me, maybe a couple of years older, and he looked tired. He has four kids at home, all under the age of ten. I told him I appreciated him coming, and he said he was sorry he missed Cliff.

He left a little while later after chatting with Ms. Nancy about all the other people they knew who were sick and in the hospital. I texted Cliff to let him know who had stopped by. His phone was at the house, but I thought he could read it after he got home.

My mom, who works in the nursing home wing of the hospital, came by before she had to start work. I was absently playing on my phone, bored with all the "who is sick and who is dying" conversation, since none of it was about people I knew.

I blurted out, "Mom, have you seen Ms. Nancy's face?"

I'm an awesome daughter-in-law, I know. And twelve.

Mom smiled and said, "Well, yes, but I wasn't going to bring it up." She sat down and chatted with Ms. Nancy for a little bit before heading back to the other wing to work.

Stanley showed up next. Stanley, our children's minister, always enters a room with a big smile. He asked about Cliff, too, and shared a couple of funny stories about going with Reggie on hospital visits and seeing way more of the patient they were there to visit than they really intended or wanted to. Stanley was perfectly happy to stay out in the waiting room with the family. Less R-rated that way.

Time passed quickly. Dr. Barnes was now back, chatting with Ms. Nancy about travel stuff. Ms. Brenda stuck her head in—she's the executive secretary for the hospital CEO and from our church too. My friend Heather, who works in the home health area of the hospital, also came for a quick visit. She gave me a hug and glanced at Ms. Nancy's face with a little questioning look at me. I choked back a smile.

Finally, the first hour of surgery was over and all the visitors were gone. Ms. Nancy picked up one of the magazines on the table and started thumbing through it while I pulled out my iPad. It wasn't long before the phone in the waiting room rang, and a nurse let me know Cliff was out of surgery and doing fine.

His doctor came wading in just a few minutes later. I say wading because that's what he was wearing—brown rubbery wader boots, clear up to his thighs, an odd-looking accessory with his bright green scrubs and scrub cap. Dr. Whatley had pictures in his hand and motioned me and Ms. Nancy over.

"OK, we're all done," he said, "and I wanted to show you what we did." He looked me in the eye. "We couldn't find a tear."

"Huh? He didn't have a tear?"

So why did we just put him through surgery?

"The MRI showed a tear, but when we got in there, I checked here and here…"

Dr. Whatley showed me microscopic images of tissue in Cliff's shoulder as he explained what he had done to be confident there was no tear, that the MRI was wrong. It was almost like looking at a sonogram but in color. In a sonogram, I might be able to make out the baby. The pictures in front of me looked like blobs. Weird, gross-looking blobs.

"We did completely remove the bone spur that was also in there. The good news with all of this is it means his recovery time will be a whole lot faster."

That was good news.

That morning, Cliff and Caleb and I had asked God to help Cliff's recovery time be quick and not too painful. I guess he was already answering our prayer.

"Anyway, he looks good, and when he's ready, the nurses will come and take you back to see him," Dr. Whatley said.

With a thanks from us, he was gone and Ms. Nancy was picking up her purse to head out and get herself some drugs for her tooth infection.

Now, I just needed to sit and wait until Cliff woke up and I could go back there.

More waiting. And a text from his brother begging me to get Cliff on video all drugged up.

VIDEO, it read.

I considered it.

When they finally took me back to see him, he was still pretty out of it. His right arm was in a sling with lots of bandaging all around his right shoulder. I bent down and gave him a kiss and pulled up a chair to sit by him.

The nurse in charge told me he needed to drink water. Apparently peeing in a cup was his ticket out of the hospital, and she seemed in a hurry to call it a day. She was ready to go.

But Cliff, my man who could sleep in until noon on a Saturday if I let him, was not. He groggily woke up just a little, enough to hear me tell him what the doctor had said. Twenty minutes later, he woke up again and asked the exact same question.

I texted his brother.

VIDEO, he texted back.

I tried a couple of times, but it was mainly of Cliff sleeping. Lame. And silly for me to even try. I felt like I was breaking a sacred trust. Something that's between the lines of your wedding vows that say "to have and to hold" and "till death do us part," that's more of a "to avoid taking embarrassing videos so your brother can make fun of you" kind of vow. I just wanted to take care of him instead.

"Is he waking up?" the nurse said, loudly, as she walked in to check on us. She handed me a clear plastic jug. "Mr. Horn, want to try going to the bathroom for me now?"

We helped him sit up slowly, his feet swinging heavily to the floor. I assisted him with his pants and his socks, and I did my best to get the oversized shirt we'd brought over the sling contraption he has on, to at least drape around him.

I had this weird feeling that this is something I expect to do when we're both in our eighties. Not necessarily right now. I think Cliff was having the same feeling. We helped him up, and I walked with him, supporting his good arm, as he shuffled to the bathroom. We stood there for what felt like ten minutes. No go.

We shuffled back, and I helped him back into the bed. I became the water drill sergeant. Every two minutes I picked up the cup with the straw and insisted he drink. Through his drug-induced fog, he looked annoyed. After another forty minutes and two pass-bys from the nurse insisting he wake up and get moving, and after I helped him with the urinal, we had urine.

The nurse started going through all the at-home care instructions with me. He has a nerve blocker—a tiny little tube they inserted into a nerve in his neck, which was giving some serious pain medication relief. There were two prescriptions I needed to fill. When I asked about the medication, she didn't give me much to go by—just that the pharmacy would answer my questions.

Then she pointed to the ice machine Cliff was hooked up to. "That will go home with you too," she said.

I immediately thought about my vegetable packs sitting in the freezer. Darn. And wondered how much the so-called convenient ice machine was going to cost. Probably more than the vegetables.

She showed me how to unhook the machine so I could change out the ice when I needed to. She went over how soon to take the nerve block out, and made sure I understood I would be the one who would have to do it. Oh, great.

We finally got the all-clear, and I went and got the car and drove it to the door where Cliff was waiting in a wheelchair. He was tired, but he managed to walk to the car with help from the nurse.

Once we got home, I walked him slowly inside and into his new room for the next week. As he got comfortable and I propped up his arm with pillows, he gave me a kiss.

"Thanks, babe, for taking care of me," he whispered as he laid his head back and started to drift off.

I smiled and kissed him back.

"Want some pain medicine?" I asked.

"Nah," my tough guy answered. "I'm good."

His tune changed about one the next morning. I am not a heavy sleeper, but I am deaf, I'm pretty sure. There are many things I can't hear, and I knew I couldn't take any chance sleeping in our room at the opposite end of the house from where Cliff was. So I'd made myself a little place on the couch in the living room and put my cell phone by my head just in case I couldn't hear Cliff call for me.

I did hear the phone ring.

"You need something?" I stumbled to Cliff's side in the dark.

"My shoulder really hurts."

"Well, you did just have surgery," I patiently pointed out.

I know, helpful.

"Want to take your pills now?" I asked.

Cliff groaned. "Yes."

I gave him his dose and in my sleepy haze, managed to pull out a marker and write down the dosage and the time on the big dry-erase board I keep in the kitchen. He was going to follow doctor's orders for the next few days and have a regular medication time. Even if it meant that I would have to get up every four to six hours to give it to him.

But that's exactly what I did. I watched his medication schedule like a hawk. I made sure he ate. During the night, I got up and changed out his ice machine and woke him up to give him his medicine.

The next day, Heather stopped by with some potato soup she'd made.

"How's he doing?" she asked as we stood in the middle of the kitchen.

"He's better," I said. "He's hurting but he's doing OK. I think it's just going to be a few more days before he starts feeling a little more like himself."

Heather smiled. "Well, I have to tell you what one of the other nurses told me yesterday."

After she'd left the waiting room, Heather had stepped into the elevator with a nurse named Kathy, who had helped with some of Cliff's pre-op work.

"Do you know the Horn family?" Kathy asked Heather, having seen her talking to us in the waiting room.

"Yeah, his wife and I are best friends, and we all go to the same church and stuff," Heather said.

"Well, they just seem to be the sweetest couple. He just couldn't stop talking about her, about how much she helped him get ready for the surgery and how she's always there for him. They just seem to really love each other a lot."

My eyes started tearing up as Heather told me what the nurse had said. It's one thing to want to believe your relationship is special, that your marriage is solid. It's another to hear about it through someone else.

Despite my exhaustion, despite feeling like I had a newborn in the house again, I found myself that second night looking at Cliff, this time at two in the morning, as he drifted back to sleep after taking the medicine I offered him. A wave of realization washed over me. Maybe it was my lack of sleep triggering this seriously emotional moment, or maybe it was just the stillness of everything that gave me greater clarity. But I had an overwhelming sense of truth.

I am absolutely in love with this man. Despite his flaws or his hang-ups or the little things he does that sometimes drive me crazy. I can't imagine him not being in my life. I can't imagine him not being by my side. I can't imagine not being by his.

Marriage is not for the merry moments. Marriage is for the moments that aren't so merry. It's the one relationship you can lean into when things go wrong. When hearts hurt, when feelings get frayed, and yes, when shoulders get sliced into and you need somebody to change the icepack.

I am my husband's helper. There is something profound and soul-stirring about the art of a man and woman brought together by their Creator, who had the idea that each of us might need the other.

Bone of his bone.

Flesh of his flesh.

I'm realizing that being his helper does not subtract from my own existence. It doesn't take away. Instead, I think it adds. Wholeness. Completeness.

Not just for me. But for both of us.

Joining together as a husband and wife cannot be measured by the world's standards where a marriage today is like a business contract that always contains a loophole or like a dinner party where if a guest gets bored or unhappy, she can just leave.

There is sanctity in the vows we say. There is holiness in the promises we make.

For better or for worse.

In sickness and in health.

There is submission.

There is obedience.

There is love.

And all three things start first with God.

I'm realizing that in my relationship with God, as I submit, as I obey, as I follow his plans and his authority over my life, that it's easier to honor Cliff as the leader of our family, as the leader of our home, and yes, as the spiritual leader of me, as my husband. And I'm realizing that as I learn, sometimes painfully, sometimes exasperatedly, to step back and let my husband have the reins, that it is a subtle, small reminder of what it means to step back and let God lead it all.

There is freedom in believing I don't have to be in control. I can let go.

I know now that there are battles that are mine to be fought, and battles I am meant only to cheer on. I do not have to lead the charge. I do not have to carry the flag.

I can simply follow.

With the gifts and talents and insights and perspectives God's given me, I follow. I offer. I serve. I help. I listen. I share. I observe. I direct. I attempt to pour, more than I try to ladle out.

And I can see the blessings.

I covered Cliff up with a blanket as the ice machine whirred and the light from the kitchen threw shadows over his sleeping face. I understand better now why marriages are supposed to last a lifetime. There is so much more to learn, and there is so much more to know.

This last year has certainly been a year of lessons. When I first began this whole experiment on submission, I wasn't sure what it would be like. I half-suspected it wouldn't work. Or that I wouldn't like it. A number of women said, "I could never do that," when I told them I was attempting to be a submissive wife.

But now, looking back, I honestly think they could do it. Because I've done it. Or I'm doing it. No, it's definitely not perfect. I've made mistakes this year, and I'm sure I'll make more mistakes in the future. But if God has taught me just one thing in all of this searching and analyzing and interpreting—it's that putting him first when it comes to my marriage will never cause me to lose. Or be a loser, for that matter. Loving Cliff God's way—by following what his Word says in honoring my husband, being intentional, and (working on) being selfless—opens a door. I'm watching Cliff lead our family with more confidence and speak up more confidently about his faith. And while I suspect the whole work-and-home balance thing will still plague me a while longer, when it comes to my role as a wife, I don't feel like I have to do it all on my own anymore. I've seen what happens when I step back and make room for my husband to step forward.

I no longer feel so alone.

I don't feel so weighed down.

I do feel lighter.

I feel free.

Discussion Questions

These questions are intended for you to use in your personal journal or to be answered as a group for your book club or Bible study group. Feel free to include your own!

1. Before reading *My So-Called Life as a Submissive Wife*, what were your thoughts about submission?

2. Do you know anyone who acts submissive in her marriage? How would you describe her? Does she match up to your original idea of submission? Why or why not?

3. How would you describe how your marriage works? How would your husband?

4. Could you relate to Sara's description of a small town? Why or why not?

5. How would you describe your relationship with your mother-in-law? Could you live with her for a year?

6. Before reading this book, would you describe yourself as submissive in your marriage? Why or why not?

7. Influence from friends can have a bigger impact on our marriages than we may think. How have your friends hindered or encouraged you in your marriage?

8. Do you see a different attitude about marriage when it comes to your grandparents' or your parents' generation compared with your own? Why or why not? How would you describe it as different?

9. Have you ever lived with your in-laws or parents after you were married? What were the biggest challenges you dealt with? What were the benefits?

10. Do you live by routines? In every part of your life, or just a few, or none? Why or why not?

11. How have you usually approached the verses in the Bible that talk about submission? Have you viewed them as currently applicable and words we need to take seriously; optional (not

necessarily a commandment but something to consider); or do you not take them seriously nor are they ever on your radar (you ignore them)?

12. Do you believe that submission to your husband must start first with looking at submission to God? Why or why not?

13. The Message version reads: "Wives, understand and support your husbands in ways that show your support for Christ." What does this mean to you? Do you agree with it? Why or why not?

14. Do you think the attitudes toward men in the workplace have affected women's attitudes toward their husbands at home? Why or why not?

15. Who's better at household responsibilities, you or your husband? Or do you take turns or split the work?

16. As Sara shares in the book, have you looked at yourself more as an individual than as a woman? Would you say you embrace being a woman or you are more likely to not think about it? Why or why not?

17. Do you view marriage as God's design to complete each other as man and woman, husband and wife? Why or why not?

18. Were you close to your grandparents? What has your grandparents' marriage taught you about marriage in general, good or bad?

19. Have you ever lived in a multigenerational home? How would you describe it? What were the benefits? What were the challenges?

20. What's the chore you always seem to be doing (and don't mind doing)? What's the chore you really wish someone else would do and you'd never miss it again?

21. TMI question (to be answered solely at your discretion and maybe just with your closest friends): Sex before breakfast? Yes? No? Only after the toothbrush has been used?

22. Where (or from whom) did you learn your earliest attitudes about sex? Do you see sex differently now that you're married? How have your thoughts and attitudes changed?

23. Have you ever been struck with the thought that you might not really need your husband? If so, how has that thought affected your actions or attitude toward him?

24. How do you view marriage? A 50/50 partnership? 100/100? If he makes me happy, I'll make him happy?

25. How do you find time to be intimate with your husband when all the other responsibilities you have (kids, house, work) clamor for your attention?

26. Have you ever made a major decision without talking to your husband about it first? What was it? What happened as a result, if anything?

27. What was your wedding like? If you were to do it all over again (with the same husband), what's one thing you would keep? What's one thing you would change?

28. Have you ever made the decision to quit something because it was impacting time for your marriage or your family? What happened?

29. What were your initial perceptions of what life would be like being married? How did those perceptions change after you got married?

30. How do you balance it all? Or do you? What do you do well? What do you wish you did better?

31. Have you ever been judged by other women for working full time outside the home? Have you ever been judged by other women for being a stay-at-home mom? How have you handled the comments or the criticism?

32. What did you think of Mamaw's story of her relationship with her husband? Do you know women with similar stories?

33. Sara mentions the picture of the elderly couple walking off together hand in hand. What do you think of the statement, "Want to know why we're still together? Because back in our day, when something was broken, you didn't throw it away. You fixed it." Is it harder to fix things today then decades ago? Why or why not?

34. Ephesians 5:24 says, "Now as the church submits to Christ, so wives are to submit to their husbands in everything." How do you interpret the word *everything*?

35. Share your thoughts about this statement: "Does my lack of trust at times actually keep my husband from embracing his God-given call as the leader of our household? Do I ever get in the way of him pursuing the role God intended for him?"

36. Was Sara right in giving up the newspaper job? Should she have stuck with it? Should she have taken it in the first place?

37. What do you think this verse means? "Wives, submit to your own husbands as to the Lord."

38. Do you agree with the idea of loving your husband HIS way (with Honor, Intention, and Selflessness)? What's the hardest part for you to do?

39. Have you and your husband ever shopped for a house? Who had final say? How did you come to a decision?

40. Who does more housework, you or your husband? Do you ever fight about housework? Did you ever discuss chores (who would do what) before you got married?

41. Have you ever had a major fight with your husband that ended with no one really winning? How did you resolve it?

42. What do you think about Sara's question, "Does God really expect me to just keep my mouth shut? What's the point of being a helper to my husband if I do that, even when I think there may be a better way or a better answer?" How would you answer that?

43. Do you agree there is a chain of command in the home? Why or why not?

44. How much do you let your husband help? How often do you find yourself complaining about the way he has helped rather than being grateful he has helped at all?

45. Have you ever made a list of how you can help your husband? What would be your top three ways?

46. Does your family do devotions together? What has helped you start? What has kept you from doing them?

47. Do you and your husband have something similar to The Hug that Cliff and Sara do? Do you think something like a twenty-second hug would benefit your marriage too?

48. Do you see your marriage as holy? Why or why not?

49. Has your husband ever gotten upset because you've spent more time with the kids than with him? How did you handle that?

50. What's one way in recent memory you've honored your husband?

51. Is reading erotic fiction or steamy romance novels OK? Do you agree with Sara on this topic? Why or why not?

52. Do you enjoy hosting others for dinner? Why or why not?

53. How has your husband surprised you? What was the best surprise gift he ever gave you?

54. Do you make a point to wait on your husband when it comes to refilling a drink or taking away a plate? Why or why not? Is this a silly custom or a small way to show you care?

55. Do you let your husband have the last word when it comes to decisions for your children? Why or why not?

56. How do you and your husband work together to provide for your household?

57. Like Sara, have you ever felt that you're struggling to do it all? How do you cope?

58. Do you think it's good to have designated responsibilities around the house? Why or why not?

59. What's one way you've found to help you stay organized?

60. Do you have an irrational fear like Sara's fear of lizards? What is it?

61. Do you ever feel overwhelmed with your role as a wife and a mom and all the other titles and hats you wear? How do you get through it?

62. Have you ever been in a challenging situation, such as a hurricane, where your husband seemed less concerned than you? How did you handle it or respond?

63. Can you relate to Sara's concern about not focusing on her family and letting other interests distract her? What have you found yourself struggling with the most?

64. Have you ever struggled with loneliness or feeling completely alone in a room full of people? How have you dealt with it?

65. Describe a time when you saw God put you right where he needed you to be.

66. What do you think—is being intentionally kind to our husbands brainwashing?

67. How do you say "I love you" to your husband? How do you show love to your husband?

68. Do skills and talents need to be considered when splitting up work, whether for the home or for something else? Why or why not?

69. Have you ever wished for your husband to make more decisions because you are more of a worrier than he is? Why or why not?

70. Do you have frequent connection with your husband's family or do you let your husband communicate with them?

71. Do you find joy in helping your husband? Or is it a struggle? Why or why not?

72. Do you struggle with waiting? Why or why not?

73. Do you agree with this statement: "Marriage is not for the merry moments. Marriage is for the moments that aren't so merry." Why or why not?

74. Is your view of submission different since reading the book? If so, in what ways?

75. What is one thing you believe you can do better to help make a difference in your marriage?

About the Author

Sara Horn is a wife, mom, author, speaker, and founder of Wives of Faith, a faith-based military wives ministry (www.wivesoffaith. org). Since 2006, Sara has encouraged and inspired military wives of all branches of service to seek God's strength over their own. Her desire is to help women everywhere see their incredible value through God's eyes, to know their distinct calling, fulfill their important roles in their families, and develop strong relationships with God.

Sara has written more than ten books, the majority as a ghost-writer or collaborator. As the wife of a Navy reservist, she had the rare privilege of traveling to Iraq twice in 2003 to report and write stories of Christians in the military—the first time on board the USS *Harry S. Truman*, the second time to Baghdad. Her first book, *A Greater Freedom: Stories of Faith from Operation Iraqi Freedom*, recorded those travels and was written with Oliver North, receiving a 2005 Gold Medallion nomination. Her most recent titles include *GOD Strong: A Military Wife's Spiritual Survival Guide*, the Bible study *Tour of Duty: Preparing Our Hearts for Deployment*, and *My So-Called Life as a Proverbs 31 Wife*.

Though for many years Sara said she'd never do women's ministry, God had other plans, and he has instilled in her a passion to encourage and speak to the hearts of women, reminding them of the hope and strength we have when we rely on him.

She currently lives in the Baton Rouge, Louisiana, area with her son and her husband, who is preparing for a third deployment.

To correspond with Sara or to request a speaking kit, contact her at sara@sarahorn.com or visit her website at sarahorn.com. You may also connect with her on Facebook at facebook.com/sara hornwrites or on Twitter (@sarahorn).

Also by Sara Horn

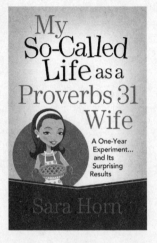

My So-Called Life as a Proverbs 31 Wife
A One-Year Experiment...
and Its Surprising Results

Sara Horn always admired the Proverbs 31 wife, but when she became a busy writer and mother, she deemed this model to be dated and impossible. Or is it? Join Sara as she heads into a one-year domestic experiment and offers full access to see if this biblical model can be embraced by a modern woman—even one who can't sew.

With humility and humor, Sara sets out to pursue the Proverbs 31 traits through immersing herself in all things domestic. But when her family's situation changes and she must return to a full-time job, she's forced to look at the Proverbs 31 woman with a whole new viewpoint. Through it all, she and readers discover:

- what it means to be a godly woman and wife
- how investing in family and faith refines priorities as a spouse and a parent
- how mistakes are opportunities for growth

This thought-provoking, surprising, and entertaining personal account will inspire women to try their own experiments in living out God's purpose for their lives.

To learn more about Harvest House books and
to read sample chapters, log on to our website:

www.harvesthousepublishers.com

HARVEST HOUSE PUBLISHERS
EUGENE, OREGON